MIND YOUR OWN *Mini* BUSINESS!

How to start your own "Mini-biz"™ with $10 to $1,000 and make all the money you need

By Will Davis

Published by The Success Team
Raleigh, North Carolina

To Marilyn, my best friend, who offered unswerving support, hundreds of helpful suggestions, and countless hours ... she also happens to be my wife.

This book is for information only and is not intended to replace legal advice. To the best of the author's knowledge, the companies mentioned in this book are reputable. However, readers are advised to conduct their own evaluation of a company before committing to one of its programs. The author does not warrant the performance of any company presented in this book, nor is the author responsible or liable for the actions of any of the companies.

Published by
The Success Team
P.O. Box 98205
Raleigh, NC 27624

ISBN 0-9629784-0-X

Table of Contents

Section I A catalog of Mini-biz opportunities 159

Section J Your final checkout 259

List of exercises

Guide to frequently asked-for information

Introduction

Today, more than ever before, people are starting their own businesses. Millions more have the dream to be on their own. The sad fact is that most people will never try. Lack of money is one of the most common reasons. So is the fear of "losing your shirt" if the business fails. There is evidence to support those fears. Various studies show that a majority of new businesses fail within the first three years, usually with major financial losses. This does not have to happen.

My goal in writing this book is to show you how to start a business with very little money—maybe with $10, maybe with a few hundred dollars, but no more than $1,000. In the title, I say you will need at least $10 to start because there is always something you will have to buy—inexpensive business cards, advertising flyers, a paint brush—whatever it might be in your case.

The title also says you can make all the money you need. I believe this is true, but you are the only person who can make it happen by following this book, selecting the right business for you, and giving it the required time and energy. Notice I say you can make all the money you need, not want. Experience shows that few people ever accumulate all the money they want because they keep raising that amount as they make more and more money.

How far can you go? That depends on a number of factors. Some businesses that started with very little money have grown to become huge corporations, such as Apple Computers, Microsoft, Pepperidge Farms, and Celestial Teas. Many other businesses have remained intentionally small, providing incomes to meet their owner's needs. These needs range from earning extra money part-time to making a million dollars a year.

In recent years, the pattern has been to require more and more money to start a business. It is common to see advertisements for a business franchise asking for "only" $15,000 to $25,000, and much more! Starting a similar business on your own, without a franchise, usually will cost you just as much. For most people, these figures mean using their life savings or accepting the burdens of borrowing.

But all is not lost. Yes, today it is still possible to start with almost nothing and GROW. Proper planning is the key to success. It will also reduce the risk of failure and the loss of money.

That is what this book is all about. It is designed for almost anyone wanting to start a small business on a limited budget—male or female, young or old, experienced or inexperienced. This is a challenge because readers have different backgrounds, interests, and abilities. You also have different reasons for wanting your own business.

I will be discussing the "Mini-biz"™ concept—businesses that will allow you to:

- Start with almost no money, up to $1,000.
- Start without quitting your present job.
- Work at home, in many cases.
- Capitalize on what you already know. If not, the business must be easy to learn.
- Operate the business full or part-time, year-round or seasonally.
- Grow the business to a much bigger business if you choose.

It is not magic. Many people have shown it can be done. Most of them will admit they are not geniuses, probably no smarter than the rest of us. However, most will also admit to a desire to learn, a determination to succeed, and a willingness to do a great deal of hard work to get started.

Although luck has helped in some cases, luck is certainly not the answer....

I am a great believer in luck. I find the harder I work the more I have of it - Thomas Jefferson

So let's get started!!

Section A
Background

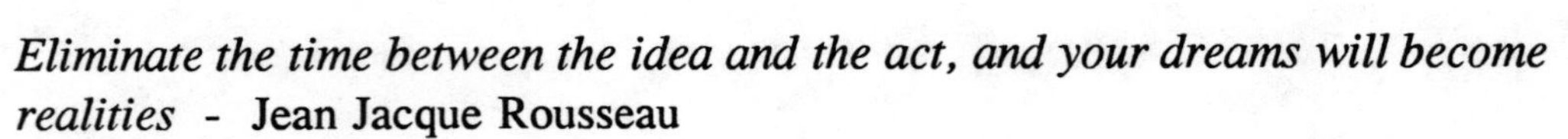

Eliminate the time between the idea and the act, and your dreams will become realities - Jean Jacque Rousseau

1 How to use this book

Use this book as a guide and reference for starting and running your own business. The book covers a wide range of topics. Don't panic! You certainly do not need to know all of this information. It is here in case you do need it, now or in the future. Some of it you may never need, depending on your business and what you already know.

Important features of this book

- This book is really two books in one. Sections A through H cover the "how-to" of selecting, starting and running a business. The Catalog of Mini-biz Opportunities, starting on Page 161, describes hundreds of specific opportunities you can consider.

- Use the checklist found in Exercise 9 at the end of the book to make sure you have covered everything you need to do to start a business.

- Whenever you get a good idea for a business, write it down in Exercise 10 at the end of the book. The exercise will help you to make the final decision on which business to start.

- I try to explain business concepts in language that most readers will understand. You will not find any fancy business terms, unless they are explained in simple language.

- This is not a cookbook with simple recipes that apply to all cases. Rather, I try to get you to think about what is best for you.

- I include a number of exercises to get you to think and learn. Be sure to do all those that apply to you and your goals in business.

If you plan to start a business soon

The best way to start is by reviewing the Table of Contents. It is your road map to guide you to the information you need. Although I have tried to keep related information together, each reader's interests and experiences will be unique. You may find yourself skipping back and forth among lessons to get the information you need in the order you need it. That's okay.

If you plan to start in the future

This book is an excellent way to learn and prepare for a future business. Take your time and study as much as you need. It is much better to learn what may happen in advance than to be faced with an unexpected crisis which requires an immediate—and expensive—solution.

Here is a tip: make your future business a current hobby. Learning now can be fun and interesting, and turn into big profits later. There is a great deal you can do now to prepare for the future. Far too many people wait until they are forced to do something—such as after being laid off—before they think about the future. This is wrong! Do it now.

What this book will not do

No book can provide all the answers. Even the simplest business can have unforeseen problems. There will be times when you may need additional help and I try to tell you where to get it.

Do not expect to become an expert just by reading this or any other book. That will only come as you work in your business. Don't worry. In most businesses you do not have to be an expert to succeed. It is only important that you are reasonably good at a number of tasks to operate a successful business.

This book is not meant to replace the professional help you might need, depending on your business. Good lawyers, accountants, and insurance agents earn their fees by protecting you from potentially bad situations. They can also save you a great deal of money. If in doubt, seek advice <u>before</u> you commit your time and money. Preventing a problem is much less expensive than correcting one.

2 Advantages of a small business

There are many advantages to having your own business. For example, you can:

- Gain financial independence.

  There are plenty of opportunities for you to make as much money as you need. The opportunities will depend on the business you select <u>and</u> the amount of effort you are willing to put into the business.

  As the business grows, it will become more valuable. In the future, you may be able to sell the business at a profit because of its "equity," or worth.

  If this will be a second job, it can provide significant extra income.

- Be your own boss - This is certainly the "American Dream."
- Avoid restrictions on age, sex, race, formal education.
- Work from your home, in many cases.
- Do what you like to do.
- Take advantage of your talents.
- Achieve significant tax advantages.
- Feel personal achievement.
- Enjoy the prestige that comes with having your own business.
- Employ family members.
- Work when you want.
- Travel.
- Have fun!

You may have additional reasons. Some reasons will be more important to you and your business than others. Some may not apply to you at all.

The simplest case

Here is the classic story of how you could start "with nothing" and build a business.

- You need money!
- You have no business experience and little money for a business.
- You start with things you find in your home. You create something in your home from inexpensive items—fabric, wood, paper and paint, food ingredients ....
- Friends like what you have made and ask to buy them.
- You are encouraged and take a few to a local store, a fair, a craft show or flea market.
- People like what they see and buy them.
- You receive orders for more.
- You hire part-time help, or contract with friends or manufacturers to make more.
- You hire sales representatives to sell your products.
- Orders pour in, and YOU ARE IN BUSINESS!

This scenario has taken place thousands of times. Many businesses have started as a hobby, or out of a need to supplement family income, or just because someone wanted something to do.

Typical products have included cookies, brownies, slippers, wooden toys, board games, birdhouses, picnic tables, jewelry, etc, etc. Mail order is another classic example of "starting on the kitchen table."

Some of these companies have remained small but very profitable. They provide enjoyable work and a comfortable living for their owners. These satisfied owners do not want additional job responsibilities or pressures.

Others have become big businesses, such as Pepperidge Farms, Famous Amos cookies, and Mattel Toys. This growth has brought with it all the problems and rewards of becoming big.

Work is more fun than fun - Noel Coward

3 Challenges of a small business

Despite the obvious advantages of having your own business, there are also potential problems that could come with <u>any</u> new business, including those I will be describing.

- You will be responsible to your creditors and customers. As you grow, you might have to worry about employees.
- Even though I will show you how to start with little money, you could still lose personal and family money if you grow too quickly without a plan.
- You could be working long hours, including nights and weekends. You might have to give up vacations for a while.
- There might be less time for your family and personal life.
- You and your family may have to do without some things you would like to have.
- Income may vary from period to period. If this is your only job, there could be periods with no income.
- You must make <u>all</u> decisions, big and small. You may carry worries wherever you go.
- You must always be selling: yourself, your ideas, your products or services to customers, suppliers, and lenders.

- There will be paperwork and business records to keep. This is especially true if you hire employees.

- You will have to perform many tasks you prefer not to do. For example, some people do not like to sell or do detail work.

- If you have people working for you, you will have to hire and fire. You will feel a responsibility for them. At the same time, you will be responsible for any mistakes they might make.

If you consider any of these to be a serious problem, you have four choices. You can:

1. Resolve to charge ahead and accept what comes.

2. Select an opportunity that reduces the chance for the problems to occur.

3. Decide to keep your company small, work at your own pace, and be satisfied with less income.

4. Prepare yourself by learning how to handle or work around the problems.

Difficulties are things that show people what they are - Epictetus

Section B

The Mini-biz™ concept

Life is not easy for any of us, but what of that? We must have perseverance, and, above all, confidence in ourselves. We must believe we are gifted in something, and that this thing, at whatever cost, must be attained - Marie Curie

4 What is a Mini-biz?

Definition of a Mini-biz™

"Mini-biz" is an quick way to say miniature business. I use this word to describe a small money-making enterprise that:

- Does not follow all the rules that a typical small business follows, and
- Can be started with very little money.

Why a Mini-biz?

Let's face it. Starting and running any business takes time and energy, and most people would accept those demands. But then there is always the unknown: how successful will the business be? If you could be absolutely sure that the business would do well, you could borrow all the money you needed, because you would know you could pay it back. You could invest every penny you had, put up your house as collateral, and borrow from friends and relatives with confidence.

But nothing in life is that certain. The more into debt you go, the more sleepless nights you will have until you have your debts under control. You will remember that cute little boutique that looked like a winner, but went out of business. And what happened to that great Chinese restaurant down the street? You wonder what happened to the owners of those businesses, and how much money they might have lost. Then the news is filled with talk about economic uncertainties. If you are conscientious, these negative concerns could take much of the fun out of being in business for yourself, and leave only worries. As a result, you do nothing.

Please do not misunderstand what I am saying. Every month, thousands of people take the risk and eventually succeed, and that's great! But, thousands of others fail, leaving themselves in debt, and that's too bad. If you could have a small business you enjoy, make good money, and not have to worry about debt or business failure, wouldn't that be nice? Or, if for some reason you were unable to borrow money, but would like to have your own business, wouldn't a Mini-biz be a good answer?

A Mini-biz versus a small business

Is there a difference between a small business and a Mini-biz? The answer is definitely yes. While a Mini-biz is a small business, the reverse may not be true. Here is a simple comparison of some significant advantages and limitations:

	Mini-biz	**Small Business**
Investment	$10 to $1,000	Thousands to millions of dollars
Opportunities	Many	Many more
In debt	Probably not	Probably
Employees	0 - 2	0 - 500
Paperwork	Some	Much more
Require legal help	Possibly	Definitely
Operate part-time	Yes	Maybe, depending on type
Business plan required	Partial	Probably (definitely, if you want to borrow money)

And so, we have the "Mini-biz" concept, designed for people who cannot or do not want to go into debt, but still want a business of their own.

Nothing can happen if not first a dream - Carl Sandburg

5 Keys to starting a Mini-biz™

There are certain rules to follow if you want to start a business with limited money.

1. **Do <u>not</u> rent a workplace**. Renting usually means signing a lease, which commits money for a long time. You might work from your home or garage. Your business might be one where you go to your customers' homes or businesses. Maybe you can sell at a flea market or fair. There you can rent a small space at a very low rate for the short period required.

2. **Do <u>not</u> hire employees**. Avoid fixed salaries and the paperwork involved. If you need help, you can start by using family members or "contractors" (more on this in Lesson 28).

3. **Do <u>not</u> incorporate**. Start as a proprietorship (you are the owner). Incorporating a business can be expensive and will cause more record keeping. In addition, you would be considered an employee of the corporation for tax purposes and your tax records would be much more complicated. Later on, as the business grows, you may want to incorporate (more on this in Lesson 21).

4. **Avoid borrowing money**. One of the purposes of a mini-biz is to give you peace of mind about debts. If you <u>must</u> borrow, keep the amount to something you could pay back in time without too much hardship.

5. **Avoid excessive expenses for equipment**. Select work based on equipment you own. For example, you can use your car, truck,

tools or personal computer. If you need equipment you do not own, consider renting until you can afford to buy. If you must buy, wait until you have a job requiring the tool.

6. **Control initial expenses.** Avoid frills—use what you have. Do not spend money for fancy desks or furnishings. Buy only what you really need. Remember, many small businesses have been started on a kitchen table.

7. **Avoid or limit inventory.** Unless you can move inventory quickly, do not tie up your money on excess inventory.

8. **Select cash-payment opportunities.** Select a business where you get paid quickly in cash. If your work will take time to complete, get a partial payment at the start. Often, this will be enough to pay the job's expenses.

9. **Go with what you know.** Avoid lengthy learning or training periods, unless you can afford to do it before you start the business.

10. **Select a business that suits your personality, skills, and experience.** You want a business where you will perform well and be comfortable.

11. **Avoid businesses with legal risks and liabilities.** Avoid products or services that could expose you to a law suit. Do not sell products that make wild, unsubstantiated claims, or that have a potential health or safety risk.

12. **Finally, put a fair amount of profits back into the business.** When you start making money, avoid the temptation to spend it for personal use. Keep some in the business to improve it and make it grow.

This is very important, so let me repeat. These rules apply when starting a business with a limited money supply; many of these rules could change as you grow.

It may be that your dream is to own a business that requires a significant investment to start. Consider raising money by starting a Mini-biz first. Save as much of your earnings as you can. Later, even if you cannot save enough, your savings record and work experience will help you to borrow more for the business you want.

6 What's the catch?

Does starting a Mini-biz with a small amount of money sound too good to be true? It can be done - but there are some limitations.

1. You cannot start all businesses this way. Many require larger outlays of money. However, there are thousands of opportunities open to you, and I describe hundreds of them in the Catalog of Mini-biz Opportunities, starting on Page 161.

2. While you may not be spending money, you still have to pay with something—your time and energy.

3. You will have to use your imagination to determine ways to get things done inexpensively. Once again, this will take time to develop and accomplish.

4. You may have to do things that you would prefer not to do. For example, for some businesses you might have to prospect for customers by telephone or by going door-to-door.

5. Starting with little money does not mean you will never have to borrow money. A major reason why small companies fail is lack of sufficient capital to operate and grow. If you plan to stay small, this may never be a problem. But if you plan to grow, be prepared to seek loans in the future. By then, you should have the experience and a track record of accomplishment to support your request.

To this list, you can add the challenges for any small business listed earlier in Lesson 3.

An optimist sees an opportunity in every calamity; a pessimist sees a calamity in every opportunity - Winston Churchill

7 How to succeed with *your* Mini-biz™

Numerous studies have estimated that a majority of new businesses close within their first three years. Not a very happy picture!

These same studies give clues to why companies fail. We know that company owners are highly motivated to succeed and are willing to work long hours. We also know many owners have set very specific goals to reach. So why do companies fail? The basic reasons are inadequate knowledge, planning, and money. Being motivated, working hard, and setting goals is not enough. In fact, working hard may not even be necessary in some businesses. Here are some important things you should do to improve your chances for success:

- Understand how much you need to know about the product or technical aspects of the business you are entering. "Technical" is used in its broadest sense. For example, the technical aspects of a restaurant business would include such things as food management, preparation, and serving. It would also include knowing about room layouts and table settings, as well as knowing potential sources for products, supplies, and equipment.

- Understand how much you need to know about the business side and record keeping. This need will vary; some businesses will require little, some a great deal.

- Make sure you understand who your typical customers are. See Lesson 16.

- Take steps to ensure potential customers will know about your business and can easily reach it. This could involve two critical factors—promoting your business, and your business location.

  Promoting your business will tell people about your business and what you are offering. See Lessons 33 and 34.

  Location can be an important way for people to become aware of your business. A good location also makes it easy for customers to get to your business place. While location is critical for some businesses, it may not be a factor for others. With the limited budget of a Mini-biz, you will have to work around possible problems with location. See Lesson 20.

- Plan ahead. Spend time anticipating what might happen and how you would cope with situations, good or bad. Either type of situation could be a real problem later on. You might wonder why you should plan for a good situation. Here is an example. Let's say it is just before Christmas and you have many orders for one of your products (good!). In fact, more orders than you can fill (bad? - maybe). Solving this problem would be money in the bank. However, if it is not solved quickly, you could lose that money, as well as many potential customers (definitely bad). The moral: Plan. In this example, select suppliers who can meet an unexpected demand.

A key point to remember is that you do not have to be an expert in all these areas—just reasonably knowledgeable. On the other hand, being seriously deficient in one area could ruin your chances.

In this lesson, I have outlined the major activities to be addressed in starting a small business. Each major activity has a number of additional steps which may or may not apply to your business. Section J, at the end of the book, includes a detailed checklist to help you consider and act upon all key steps.

Practice does not make perfect...perfect practice makes perfect -
Vince Lombardi

8 Other choices you have

Of course, a Mini-biz is not the only way to start. If you have a great deal of money, you could start a much larger business than a Mini-biz. When people think about going into business, they often consider borrowing money or buying a franchise. Let's discuss these two options.

Borrowing

In Lesson 4, I discussed the worries that come with debt, the major reason why many people do not like to borrow. Although borrowing money is a common practice when starting a business, you can eliminate or simplify this usually critical step by limiting your initial investment. In this way, you may already have the necessary money, or you could accumulate it by saving, or you could borrow it from a number of sources, including family members or friends. This is one reason why I concentrate on those businesses that require only a small investment.

If you want to start a business that requires a great deal of money, you may have to work hard to get a loan. If you have read anything about business loans, you probably have one of two opinions: they are easy to get—or—they are difficult, if not impossible to get. Depending on who you are, what you own, your credit history, and what you know, either statement could be correct.

If you believe it is easy, it could be for several reasons. These could include having family or friends who are willing to help. It also might be that you have enough assets and have good relations with your bank so that they will loan you the money based on your record. Getting loans in these situations is relatively easy.

But business loans from banks, government agencies, or private venture capitalists are not always easy to get. You <u>must</u> do your homework.

You must show you are a good credit risk. You must have a detailed business plan, showing where you are with your business and where you are planning to go. You must demonstrate to potential lenders that you can manage a growing and profitable company. All this takes time and in-depth knowledge of several business areas. If this does not bother you, there will be a much wider choice of businesses for you to consider than we will be discussing. In fact, this book is probably not for you.

I assume that my readers cannot or do not want to start by borrowing heavily. Some readers do not want to live with the risk and worry that could come with a loan. Others could have difficulty getting a loan because of their credit history or insufficient assets.

Why not buy a franchise?

There has been a great deal of attention given to franchising. If you have been looking for a business opportunity, you probably have investigated several of them and discovered why I do not cover them in any depth. The main reason is <u>investment cost</u>. Most franchises require much more money than I am expecting readers to commit. A relatively small percentage of franchises require an initial investment of less than $5,000. More require $15,000 to $25,000, and some $100,000 and up.

A franchise is a packaged program offered by a company to individuals, who usually pay an initial charge and then a monthly fee based on percentage of sales. In exchange, the company allows the individual to use the company name, sell its products, and benefit from national advertising.

There is no question that a franchise can be a great way to start your own business. Not only do franchises provide established products or services, but a good one will give you all the information and guidance needed to start and grow. Many people are making a comfortable living this way, and some have made fortunes.

On the other hand, a franchise does not guarantee success. There are many sad stories of people losing everything in a bad program. Because of problems in the past, federal regulations have been enacted to protect possible investors. However, misrepresentations still occur, and you would be wise to thoroughly investigate a company's history, reputation, and claims before getting involved. By law, the franchising company must provide this information.

Section C

Your opportunities and options

All this struggling and striving to make the world a better place is a mistake; not because it isn't a good thing to improve the world, if you know how to do it, but because striving and struggling is the worst way to go about doing anything -

George Bernard Shaw

9 This world of opportunities

I'll bet this has happened to you. You see a new business or product and say "why didn't I think of that?" There is a good chance you did not because you were not looking for opportunities. You also might have said, "Heck, I thought of that a long time ago!" Well, why didn't you do something with the idea?

It is not too late. Just open your eyes. Look for opportunities—then take action. There are still plenty of ways you can help people AND make money.

Life in these United States

In the United States, there are:

- 29 million people over 65 years of age. Almost 9 million live alone. How many need special care, something to do, companionship?

- 35 million working women. How many need easier meal preparations, help with home cleaning, help with children, help with shopping and clothes alterations?

- 45 million children attending elementary or high schools. How many children are at home after school by themselves? How many need something to do, help with homework, a skill or second language?

- 144 million cars. How many need minor repairs, windshield repairs, paint touchup?
- 66 million homes (3.6 million bought each year). How many need simple repairs, windows cleaned, lawn and yard work, new draperies or carpets?

And Americans are busy:

23 million play golf.

17 million play tennis.

52 million take care of their lawns.

31 million are fishermen.

22 million are hunters.

35 million own dogs.

27 million own cats.

Change: translating trends into opportunities

I am sure you agree that these facts are very interesting. But you may ask what they have to do with starting a business. Well, these facts tell me that today's opportunities are everywhere, and that new opportunities are created by change, in living, eating, and buying patterns. Here are just a few examples:

Changing population and lifestyles. We need more products and services for the elderly, children in day care, single parent families, and the increasing number of working women, to name a few.

Each of these groups provides a number of opportunities. For example, because more women work, we need more:

Day care facilities.

After-school and summer vacation activities and supervision for school-age children.

Professional clothing.

Grooming aids.

Convenience and take-out foods.

Home cleaning assistance.

It also means that more women:

Are interested in improving themselves professionally.

Want to learn how to manage their time.

Have their own discretionary funds.

Are making major purchases, such as cars.

Are shopping and doing home chores at night and on weekends.

New technologies and products. The personal computer, for example, has created thousands of businesses in manufacturing, sales, servicing, programming, application development, system design and installation, training, supplies, furniture, printers, scanners, and on-and-on-and-on.

Concern for physical fitness. We see more health clubs, health-food stores, and restaurants. We see special shoes and clothing for aerobics, walking, running, cycling—just about any sport.

Many alert and imaginative people have seen trends developing and have started a business to meet a growing need. Unfortunately, many more people who claim they want to do something are still only dreaming. With this book, I will try to get you going—and in the right direction.

There is nothing permanent except change - Heraclitus

He who refuses to embrace a unique opportunity loses the prize as surely as if he had failed - William James

10 Four ways to select a Mini-biz

If you do not know what Mini-biz you would like to start, there are four ways you can approach your search. For now, let's outline them. Later, we will be going into details. You can:

- Use a low-cost program offered by an established company.
- Copy or modify an idea used by another company.
- Create a business from something you know.
- Develop your own idea for a business.

Whenever you get a good idea for a business, write it down in Exercise 10 at the end of this book. The exercise will help you to make the final decision on which Mini-biz to start.

Use a low-cost program offered by an established company

There are companies looking for people to participate in ready-to-go programs to sell or assemble their products. In these programs, the company does not employ you, but you act as an independent agent or distributor. Your pay is based on the number of products you sell or make.

Sales opportunities

In some cases, you sell the company's products and do not have to worry about inventory. In other cases, the company sells you its products at special low prices. You then sell the products to your customers at retail. Companies offering programs range in size from small and generally unknown businesses to large and well-known corporations, such as Avon, Shaklee, and Tupperware.

There are several advantages to working with this type of company:

- You can select a program that suits you and your needs.
- In many cases, no experience is necessary.
- Most programs require little or no startup expenses.
- Often, you can start to earn money immediately.
- They will help you to start and grow.
- Your credibility is helped by their record and products.
- You have someone to contact about a problem. Their success depends on your success.
- Many companies will handle most of the business aspects for you.

Work-at-home opportunities

Companies are looking for people to work at home. The companies provide the basic materials. You put them together, return them to the company, and get paid for each assembled product. There is usually no need for expensive equipment (you may need a sewing machine for cloth products).

WARNING: Watch out for unscrupulous companies advertising home programs such as product assembling or "envelope stuffing." Check any opportunity carefully before committing. Your best opportunity may be to find a local company that offers at-home work programs. For more information on this, see Catalog C6.

Copy or modify an idea used by another company

If you see a business that is just what you would like to do, do it! There is nothing to say you cannot copy someone else's idea as long as it does not involve patents, copyrights, or other legally protected business assets.

In fact, copying is a very common activity in most businesses. Look at women's fashions or the number of different companies selling soap products. Companies in an industry go after the same customers; each hopes to attract the customer by offering better products. Even protected ideas, such as patents and copyrights, are subjected to intense and expensive review by a company if it wants to copy another company's idea.

If you want to try this approach in a small city, look for businesses in other cities to copy. It probably does not make sense to offer the same business as someone else in the same neighborhood unless you are reasonably sure there is enough business for both of you.

This approach has some advantages:

- Before committing, you can watch the other company to determine if the idea is successful.

- You can think of ways to improve on what the other company is doing.

- If you are not in the same area as the other business, the owners might help you if you are honest with them and seek their advice.

- There are many "How-to" books and manuals written by owners of successful small businesses. These can provide you with valuable knowledge before you start. In the Catalog of Mini-biz Opportunities, some of these manuals are mentioned along with a summary of the opportunity.

The next lesson will provide more information on sources for business ideas.

Create a business from something you know

Can you turn what you know into a business? Maybe you can. Here are several examples of how it might happen.

- You have worked for a company and have become an expert in a field, let's say quality control. Why not consider becoming a consultant and offer your expertise to other companies? Two cautions:

1. Sell only your expertise. Never, never, never sell or capitalize on confidential information you might know about your previous employer. At a minimum, it is unethical. It could be unlawful.

2. If you are still working for a company but are looking for part-time work, select a different business unless your management approves of your plans. Companies may not mind your moonlighting. But most will not want you using the expertise they have given you to be used for another company's gain, especially if it is a competitor.

- If you have been working in a trade, why not work on your own, taking on small jobs? There are plenty of opportunities here because many companies do not want small, less profitable jobs. As an independent with no overhead expenses, you could do the job, charge less, and still make more than you would on salary.

- You have a hobby in which you have become an expert. Why not turn that expertise into money? For example, you might teach children or an adult education class. You could write a book or publish a newsletter. If it is a hobby where you collect things (stamps, coins, books, antiques, etc.), why not spend more time buying and selling them for profit?

Develop your own idea for a business

While this is the most creative approach, it also has the most risk attached to it. Because of the unknowns, it is wise to proceed with caution. Conduct your own "market research" as part of your marketing plan to increase your chances for success (see Lesson 18). If you have a good idea, this approach has several advantages:

- A chance to be in on the beginning of a new business area with

  Less competition

  Excellent growth potential

- A high degree of personal satisfaction

For more on this approach, see Lesson 12.

11 Sources of ideas for your Mini-biz

The type of Mini-biz you select may be key to your success. If you need ideas for a business, there are a number of places you can look. As I will say many times, it is important that you keep looking for opportunities until you find the one you want. There are hundreds of sources for ideas. Here are some of the best, and where you can find them:

- **Yourself**. Keep a list of things that bother you, or you would like to see improved. Is there a business opportunity hidden there?

- **Family and friends**. During conversations, listen for what is bothering them. Ask them if they have ideas for a business.

- **Small business owners in your community**. Join civic and other community groups. Talk to these new friends and some good ideas may be generated.

- **The "Yellow Pages" telephone directories of big cities**. Most established businesses advertise there. You will see hundreds of ideas, some new, some old. Can you start one of these in your town or neighborhood? Your library may have copies of directories from some of the larger cities.

- **Business magazines and newspapers**. *Fortune, Forbes, Business Week*, and the *Wall Street Journal* report on new trends and activities in the business world. Check at your local library and get in the habit of spending time there.

- **Small Business magazines.** *Entrepreneur, Inc, Venture, and Success* report on small businesses and their problems. I especially recommend *Entrepreneur* because it describes many opportunities for the person looking to start. You can find these magazines in libraries, or you can buy recent issues at larger magazine stands. You can obtain subscription information for *Entrepreneur* by writing Entrepreneur Subscription Department, P.O. Box 50368, Boulder, CO 80321.

- **Opportunity Magazines.** Many of these magazines have good articles and advice on new business opportunities. Unfortunately, most of these magazines are loaded with advertisements for questionable get-rich-quick schemes. If intrigued, read the ads carefully and screen them. Remember the classic advice, "If it sounds too good to be true, it probably is."

  Usually, libraries do not have opportunity magazines, but you can often find them at larger newsstands. You can also get subscription information—and possibly a free copy—by writing to the publishers. Here are several of them:

  Extra Income, P.O. Box 543, Mt. Morris, IL 61054

  Income Opportunities, 380 Lexington Ave., New York, NY 10017

  New Business Opportunities, Subscription Dept., P.O. Box 58932, Boulder, CO 80306

  Small Business Opportunities, Harris Publications, 1115 Broadway, New York, NY 10010

  Spare Time Money Making Opportunities, 5810 W. Oklahoma Avenue, Milwaukee, WI 53219

- **Libraries and book stores.** They carry a variety of books on starting and operating a small or home business. These are very popular topics, and new books are being published regularly.

  Here's a tip. Before buying or taking out a book, look it over carefully. Many books dealing with small businesses and entrepreneurs are written for companies much bigger than you are interested in at this time, some even requiring millions of dollars. For now, stick to the basics for starting a small operation.

- **"How-to" books.** There are dozens of books describing how to start a particular business. You will find some in libraries or book stores. Many are sold by mail order through magazine advertising.

  WARNING: Many of the mail-order "books" are poorly written and incomplete. Some advertise questionable schemes with the promise of easy money for very little work. On the other hand, there are some excellent books available. Unfortunately, when you buy through the mail, you cannot tell which ones are worthwhile. Follow these tips when you buy:

  1. Buy from reputable companies.

  2. Only buy if there is a money-back guarantee. (Sorry, even with a guarantee there are a few companies that will ignore your request for a refund.)

  3. Keep a record and receipts for what you buy, and when.

  4. Remember what I said earlier, "If it sounds too good to be true, it probably is."

  I have found the following companies to be excellent sources for quality books that may interest you. Write for catalogs: The New Careers Center, 1515 - 23rd Street, P.O. Box 339, Boulder, CO 80306, and Betterway Publications, P.O. Box 219, Crozet, VA 22932.

- **Books describing franchise opportunities.** There are several of these books published, and you probably can find at least one in your local library. While most franchises will be beyond your budget, studying these books may give you an idea for a business you may be able to start without the franchise. What you will be missing, and not paying for, is the company name and the additional advice and support provided with the franchise.

- **"How-to" business guides.** *Entrepreneur* magazine sells more than 150 complete guides, each describing in detail how to start and operate a different small business. While most of these businesses as described will require more startup money than the $1,000 allowed for a Min-biz, you can still learn a great deal about a particular business. Guides are priced from $30 to $70. See advertisements in any issue of the magazine, or write

Entrepreneur, 2392 Morse Avenue, P.O. Box 19787, Irvine, CA 92713. Another source for this type of small business guide is National Business Library, P.O. Box 21957, Santa Barbara, CA 93121. If you are interested in being a consultant to people on a number of financial problems, write to American Institute of Consumer Credit, P.O Box 145087, Coral Gables, FL 33114.

- **New Business opportunity fairs**. These have become very popular, and are being run in many cities. You will be able to meet and talk with representatives of companies offering programs to people like you. Watch for advertisements in your local newspaper.

- **Business opportunity advertisements** in newspapers and magazines. Most local newspapers and the magazines named above have classified ad sections. Depending on the publication, you may find listings for business opportunities, products for sale, and opportunities for sales agents. The Sunday edition of *The New York Times* often has interesting "Business Opportunities" and "Merchandise for Sale" sections in its classified advertising section. Your local library may have copies.

- **Trade and industry publications**. If you have experience in a business, you are probably aware of at least one magazine or newspaper for that type of business. There are thousands of trade publications, covering almost any industry you can name. If you are interested in an industry that is new to you, visit your local library. It will have books listing all magazines published in the United States, such as the *Gale Directory of Publications and Broadcast Media*, published by Gale Research, Detroit, MI.

- **Trade Shows**. If you happen to live near a city that is hosting a trade show of interest to you, try to attend. This may be difficult because some shows take rigorous steps to restrict attendance to people in the trade. For some, a business card will get you in.

Whenever you get a good idea for a business, write it down in Exercise 10 at the end of this book.

Discovery comes to the prepared mind - Louis Pasteur

12 How to create a *new* business opportunity

<u>You</u> can create a new business opportunity. I guarantee that at some time you have had an idea for a new business or product. Think for a moment. How many times have you said to yourself, "I wish I could buy a widget that would do ________." Or, "I wish I could find someone who could fix _______ for me."

The major difference between most people and the inventor or entrepreneur is that most of us <u>wish</u> for things to happen while they <u>make</u> things happen. The idea is just the beginning—an important one—but it simply is not enough. The U.S. Patent Office states there are two critical requirements to secure a patent:

- The idea must be new, novel, and useful .... AND
- It must be "reduced to practice." The inventor must provide details or a working model to prove that the invention will really do what he or she said it would.

To these, the business world adds several more requirements before an idea has real value.

- It must be brought to the marketplace and sold.
- It must bring in anticipated revenue, or money.
- It must make a good profit.

You can see that "doing" is absolutely required, and much of this book is devoted to what has to be done. For now, let's spend some time on developing the first step—the idea.

Who says you are not creative?

If you did not demonstrate some creativity, you could not survive on your own. Many of the simplest decisions we make every day require us to be creative to some degree. Want proof?

- Did you ever lose your way?
  Did you finally get to your destination?

- Did you ever lose or run out of money to get home?
  Did you get there anyway?

Enough said. At the time, you probably felt some embarrassment and panic. You had to be creative in the process of deciding what to do next. Your mind probably raced through a number of options because you needed a solution. You may have thought of some of those options for the first time. Now I am not suggesting that we are all equally creative. On the other hand, do not sell yourself short. Give yourself a chance, and I guarantee you will be pleasantly surprised.

How to collect and analyze ideas

If you talk to creative people—inventors, writers, artists—they will tell you that the creative process is not something they can turn on and off. There are times when they are more creative than others, and good ideas may come at any time. The most important thing you can do is to train yourself to be creative. Sound complicated? Not really. Here is what to do, in two phases.

Phase 1: Collecting ideas

1. **Change your way of thinking**. Get in the habit of asking yourself, "Is there an opportunity here?" Do not be negative or rule out ideas that appear to be too difficult. Keep an open mind. Not all your ideas will be good or practical, but you need only one that is good!

2. **Open your eyes**. Get in the habit of observing what is going on around you. Once you start to look, you will be amazed at how many opportunities you will see. In your home and as you shop, note the things that bother you, or you would like improved. Remember the old adage, "necessity is the mother of invention."

3. **Listen**. Keep alert for opportunities during conversations with people in business, family members and friends.

4. **Watch for new trends**. Note new products and businesses. Watch for fads and trends—they can lead to many opportunities. For example, when jogging became popular, it created a demand for special shoes and clothes, new magazines, newsletters, and jogging clubs. We even saw new products such as shoe insoles, head bandanas, drinks, timing watches, and on and on. You can be sure that those who made money from the trend saw it coming and got involved early.

5. **Write it down**. Carry a small notepad with you, and keep one by your bed and in your car. A small, inexpensive tape recorder is better and safer to use in your car while driving. Keep a record of your ideas and things that impress you. Do not trust your memory.

Phase 2: Analyzing ideas

1. **Spend time reviewing your notes**. Concentrate on the problems for which you believe you have a possible solution.

2. **Practice "What if...?"** What if I could do this cheaper, easier, faster ....

3. **Combine two or more ideas** to make something new. For example, let's assume you have car-repairing skills. If you:

    - **Have a truck**, you can offer "service on wheels," and go to your customer's office or home to make repairs.

    - **Can work nights**, you can offer "night owl" service for busy people.

    - **Can work weekends**, you can offer weekend service for people who need their cars during weekdays.

    - **Live near a mall**, you can offer an oil change and lube service while car owners shop.

    Get the idea?

4. **Broaden your thinking.** There is a well-known marketing slogan: "Find a need and fill it." This is excellent advice, but I believe it should go further. I say, "Find or create a need and fill it." Let me explain. For more than 50 years, blue jeans were sold as inexpensive, durable work pants. Then the high fashion designers got involved. They made minor styling modifications, put their labels on the outside, and charged two to four times more. Did they find a need or create it? I would argue that they created the need, although some marketing wizards and psychologists might disagree. Did we "need" the hula hoop or the pet rock? Millions of each were sold. Again, I would argue that the need was created. Broadening your thinking can make the unusual happen.

5. **Focus on your best ideas.** When you have a good idea with a possible solution, focus on it. Spend the time it takes to decide if it really is good and if you have a workable solution.

The point of these exercises is to open your thinking to the opportunities around you. Keep in mind that needs are constantly changing, which can lead to more opportunities.

Whenever you get a good idea for a business, write it down in Exercise 10 at the end of this book.

The rewards in business go to the person who does something with an idea - William Benton

Section D

Starting the selection process

One's philosophy is best expressed, not in words, but in the choices one makes in daily living - Eleanor Roosevelt

13 Learning about yourself

So far, you have been learning about the many opportunities there are for you to succeed on your own. Now, let's start learning about the most important person in your future Mini-biz—you!

While I can write about your opportunities, I cannot write about you. Only you can do that. But we can work together so that when we are finished you will better understand yourself, your environment, and your desires. This information will help you to select a Mini-biz in which you will be both comfortable and successful.

In the past, many exercises and questionnaires have been developed to determine if you would be a successful entrepreneur. For my readers, some of these exercises could be downright frightening because they are designed for someone interested in heading a "small business" as defined by the U.S. government's Small Business Administration. The business could be a multi-million dollar operation with as many as 500 employees! For your Mini-biz exercises, I follow the "keep it simple" rule.

On the following pages, there are three self-evaluation exercises to help you look at:

- **Yourself**. The talents, experience, and interests you have. (Exercise 1)

- **What you can give your Mini-biz**. The resources and time you can give. (Exercise 2)

- **What you want from your Mini-biz**. Why you want a Mini-biz, and what you expect to get out of it. (Exercise 3)

A helpful tip for doing the exercises

I recommend that you use a pencil when you do the exercises throughout this book. This will allow you to make changes easily. Conditions are constantly changing and you may want to adjust your plans to take advantage of new circumstances.

People are always blaming circumstances for what they are. I don't believe in circumstances. The people who get on in this world are the people who get up and look for the circumstances they want, and, if they cannot find them, make them - George Bernard Shaw

Exercise 1 | Personal factors to consider

1. What important personal traits do you have?

The following list describes some personal traits that could be important in a Mini-biz. Please note that this is a basic list. Others may be required for certain businesses. For example, creativity is required in artistic enterprises. I have left space to add this type of trait if you need it for your business.

In the left column, check the boxes for the traits you have. To test a Mini-biz against the list, use the right box to check the traits the business requires. If you are fortunate, when you finish this comparison you will have a match between your traits and the ones required for your business. If you do not know what Mini-biz you want at this time, you can come back to this when you do.

Left box: You have this trait
Right box: Trait is needed for the business you have selected

- ☐ ☐ In reasonably good health
- ☐ ☐ Self motivated
- ☐ ☐ Make decisions easily
- ☐ ☐ Patient
- ☐ ☐ Persistent
- ☐ ☐ Determined
- ☐ ☐ Enthusiastic
- ☐ ☐ Work well with people
- ☐ ☐ Have a positive attitude about yourself
- ☐ ☐ Set goals, and focus on them during disappointments
- ☐ ☐ Pay attention to details
- ☐ ☐ Plan and make good use of personal time
- ☐ ☐ Have a pleasant personality and appearance

Other traits you think would be important for a business. List:

- ☐ ☐ ______________________________
- ☐ ☐ ______________________________

Exercise 1

Do you have most of these traits? While they are all desirable, it is not necessary to have all of them to be successful in a small business. They are not in any particular order because importance will vary among different businesses. In fact, some may have no importance in the Mini-biz you select. You will have to make that decision.

2. What work experience do you have?

List all significant experiences.

Technical ______________________________

____

____

Business ______________________________

____

____

3. What other basic skills and talents do you have?

List skills acquired at home, through club participation, and at school.

Take your time here if you do not have much paid work experience. As a parent, housewife, club member, or student, you have developed certain skills and have been involved with other people. Decide which of these experiences would be helpful in a business. For example, managing finances for a family, if done well, could suggest you can handle financial matters. If you tend to acquire leadership roles in clubs or schools, you probably have "people skills" that could be important.

____

____

____

____

____

Exercise 1

4. What are your hobbies?

There are thousands of cases where hobbyists have turned their skills into a business.

____

____

____

5. What other things do you like to do?

____

____

____

6. Where do you live?

Your town and neighborhood could influence your decision on a business opportunity. Check the statements that apply to yours.

Area	* Characteristics
☐ Big city	Provides a broad customer base. Transportation can be a problem.
☐ Small city	Easier to use your car, usually fewer zoning restrictions.
☐ Suburbs	Good location for house improvement businesses. You can use your car. Some zoning restrictions.
☐ Rural	Few zoning restrictions. Trucks are less of a problem. Customers need a car to get to you.

* The characteristics listed on this and the next page are not perfect definitions, but suggest typical conditions which can vary from community to community. They are provided to help you as you think about and select your future business.

Exercise 1

<u>**Your housing**</u>	<u>**Characteristics**</u>
☐ House	You can have a home office with outside parking.
☐ Apartment	A home office may be a problem. Can you work away from the apartment?
☐ Farm	More room to work. Fewer zoning restrictions. Offer farm services?

7. What is the condition of the economy where you intend to sell?

	<u>**Characteristics**</u>
☐ Prosperous	Customers have money. You can sell higher-priced products and services. Help might be scarce.
☐ Average	Concentrate on basics, although higher-priced items may sell.
☐ Below average	Stick with the basics.

8. What about your family?

Before starting a business, you should understand its possible effects on your family. Your spouse's opinions should be part of your decision. You could be working long or unusual hours, and you might be using money planned for family use. At times, you may want family members to help in the business.

- ☐ Single
- ☐ Married
  - ☐ Spouse supports your plan for a business.
  - ☐ Spouse understands you may have less time for family.
  - ☐ Spouse can help you with the business, if needed.

- ☐ Dependent children
  - ☐ Children can help with the business, if needed.

There is only one success—to be able to live your life in your own way -
Christopher Morley

Exercise 2 — What can you give to your Mini-biz?

Aside from your talents and experience (reviewed in the last section), there are certain other things you may have to give to—or use for—your business.

1. How much money can you put into your business?

☐ You have money you can afford to commit toward starting your business.
The amount you have is $ _______

☐ If necessary, you could probably commit more of your own money later.
The amount you could commit is $ _______

☐ You have sources for additional money, if needed.

List possible sources ____

____

____

Money can be a major problem for a new business. If you follow this book's plan, you may never need additional money. However, it is a good idea to review your financial situation before you start. It could avoid a potential crisis later, when it might be more difficult to resolve.

2. What tools or equipment do you own that could be used in the business?

To start your business, certain equipment might be helpful, if not necessary. To meet the money limits of a Mini-biz, you cannot afford to buy expensive equipment before starting. On the other hand, you can use equipment you already own.

Listed below are some examples of equipment that could be important in certain businesses. In the left box, check equipment you own. When you want to test a business against this list, use the right box to check the equipment the business requires. Or, you can use the list in reverse order. If you know what Mini-biz you intend to start, check the equipment you would need in the right column. Then check the left column if you have the equipment.

Exercise 2

You have this equipment
You need this equipment for the Mini-biz you have selected

☐ ☐ Car
☐ ☐ Van or station wagon
☐ ☐ Truck
☐ ☐ Personal computer
☐ ☐ Quality printer for personal computer
☐ ☐ Business typewriter
☐ ☐ Copier
☐ ☐ Facsimile (Fax) machine
☐ ☐ Sewing Machine
☐ ☐ Camera
☐ ☐ Video camera
☐ ☐ Tools of your trade
☐ ☐ Office space
☐ ☐ Large room

Other: List

☐ ☐ ______________________________

☐ ☐ ______________________________

☐ ☐ ______________________________

If you want to proceed with a Mini-biz that requires equipment you do not own, you must have an answer to this problem before proceeding. You have several choices. Can you check one of them?

☐ Arrange to borrow when needed
☐ Rent when needed
☐ Lease

3. Where would you like to work?

☐ At home
☐ Away from home

Depending on where you live or the Mini-biz you select, this may not be a problem.

Exercise 2

4. When could you work with your Mini-biz?

Check off at least one in each group:

☐ Year-round
☐ Seasonal or part of year

☐ Weekdays
☐ Weekends

☐ Normal work-time ("9-to-5")
☐ Days, part-time
☐ Evenings
☐ Late-night

These factors could affect your family and personal life. If this is a second job, allow enough time for life beyond working. If it is your only work, make sure its hours do not conflict completely with those of other activities you enjoy.

Faraway, there in the sunshine, are my highest aspirations. I may not reach them, but I can look up and see their beauty, believe them, and try to follow where they lead -
Louisa May Alcott

Exercise 3 | What do you want from your Mini-biz?

This exercise will help you to understand clearly why you want your own business. It will also help you to select one that satisfies your needs. For each question, check the statements that best describe your situation and goals.

1. Why do you want your own business?

☐ **You need money:** Money is the most important reason.
- ☐ Can't get a job
- ☐ Must stay home
- ☐ Cannot work a full day or regular hours for personal or health reasons
- ☐ Working, but need more money
- ☐ Have income, but need more money

☐ **Money is not the only reason:** (and may not even be important).
- ☐ Would like to be "your own boss"
- ☐ Can use the extra money
- ☐ Want to work at home
- ☐ Some day, would like to quit present job
- ☐ Some day, would like to retire, but make more money
- ☐ Want to use experience, talents, or skills
- ☐ Want to learn or improve certain skills (for example, selling)
- ☐ Want a feeling of accomplishment
- ☐ Want something to do
- ☐ Would like to help others
- ☐ Want to meet people
- ☐ Other ____

  ____

If you need money, you will be inclined to look for a business that will pay off quickly. If there is a potential to make a great deal of money, you might be willing to start with something you would rather not do. For example, people have gone into a selling business even though they did not like to sell. However, with success, many of these people now thoroughly enjoy what they are doing. Making money made the difference. This would not have happened if these people were not forced to try selling.

Exercise 3

If making money is not a critical factor, you may be more inclined to select a business which suits your interests and personality.

2. Do you know the type of business you would like to start?

☐Yes ☐No

If you remember your school days, you tended to get better grades in the classes you liked. Some people would argue that the situation works the other way: that is, you tend to like the classes in which you received better grades. Whichever is correct, the fact remains that we prefer to work at something we like to do and where we have confidence in our abilities. Craft shows around the country are just one example of how people are making money doing what they like to do. Business consultants, house painters, artists, and authors all sell their experience and expertise. If possible, select a business you know you will enjoy.

What you would like to do is

____

____

____

If you do not know what you would like to do:

If you have studied lessons 9 through 12 and still do not have an idea for a business, do not despair. In the Catalog of Mini-biz Opportunities, starting on page 161, I describe hundreds of real opportunities for you to consider. Many of the opportunities give the names and addresses of companies who are looking for people just like you.

3. How much money do you want to make annually?

After 1 year: $ _______

After 3 years: $ _______

You should write specific dollar amounts, but do not be too quick to enter them. First, think about your financial reasons for wanting the business. With that, you

Exercise 3

should be able to determine what amount of money would meet your financial needs, large or small. If you believe in goal setting, you know the importance of being specific. Without specific goals, you could end up just drifting along. In addition, specific dollar amounts can help you select a business. The amount of money you can make could vary dramatically depending on the business you start.

4. What growth do you want for your business?

- ☐ Operate for a specific time, then close
- ☐ Stay small
- ☐ Grow modestly, maybe hire some help
- ☐ Grow into a large business

In Lesson 37, I discuss your options for growth once you have established your business. Your growth plans could be an important factor in selecting a business.

Blessed is the man who has found his work; let him ask no other blessedness -
Thomas Carlyle

Section E
Testing your choices

Keep on going and chances are you will stumble on something, perhaps when you least expect it. I have never heard of anyone stumbling on something while sitting down - Charles F. Kettering

14 Where to get help

Let's face it. You are going to have questions and problems at the start and as your business grows. Chances are that whatever your problem is, someone else has faced it and solved it before you. Of course, finding that "someone else" can be another problem. But do not despair. There is plenty of help if you are willing to ask. Even better, much of it is free!

Sources for free help

U.S. Small Business Administration (SBA). The SBA offers a number of services for small businesses. It has offices throughout the country. Services vary, from individual counseling, to sponsoring workshops, to helping qualified persons get business loans. It also has a series of excellent booklets on various aspects of starting and operating a small business. Ask for its latest list of available booklets. The SBA also provides assistance and advice for some special groups, including women and socially and economically disadvantaged persons.

I must caution you that the federal government's definition of small business is much broader than you might expect. For example, a small manufacturing company can have up to 500 employees and a small retailer can have annual sales of up to $7.5 million. These figures are a long way from your endeavor! So the amount of help you will get at your local SBA office will depend on the individual counselors and how much time they might have to help you.

You can find the nearest office in telephone books in the U.S. Government listings.

The **Service of Retired Executives (SCORE)**. SCORE has more than 12,000 retired business executives who volunteer their time to help small businesses with their problems. They work closely with the SBA to provide much of the counseling and workshops. You can find the nearest SCORE office in the phone book under U.S. Government - Small Business Administration.

The federal **Internal Revenue Service (IRS)**. Although we usually consider them to be the bad guys, the IRS has a number of excellent publications that try to lead you through the labyrinth of tax regulations. IRS Publication 910, "Guide to Free Tax Services," lists all of their free services as well as their free tax publications. Get a copy from your local office, or call 1-800-829-3676 (1-800-TAX-FORM). You can also order other IRS publications from this number. For a list of many of the more important publications, see the end of Lesson 26.

You can contact your local IRS office for tax advice. There are also regional toll-free phone numbers you can call. Look in your phone book. Warning! Try to stay away from January 15 to April 15. Tax time causes an avalanche of calls.

The IRS also conducts day-long seminars on a variety of tax topics. Contact your local IRS office for scheduled seminars.

Other Government Resources. If you have questions regarding a specific industry or region, you can contact agencies such as the following:

- Department of Commerce
- Department of Agriculture
- Bureau of Census
- Federal Trade Commission
- Government Printing Office, Washington, DC 20402

Each of these agencies has a number of publications and staffs to provide information. If you cannot find the nearest office in the phone book under U.S. Government, try your local library.

State and municipal agencies. Although there is no consistency from state to state, all states are eager to provide aid to businesses. Most states have departments to aid small businesses, but the name of the department may vary. Some states and cities also have programs for minorities and disadvantaged people. Check your phone book under state or local government.

Colleges, technical, and business schools. These can be valuable sources for three types of information:

- Some offer non-credit courses for people interested in starting a business. Others offer courses covering specific business, technical, and trade topics.

- Some sponsor classes and workshops taught by local experts. These can be a single class focusing on one topic to a series of classes covering many topics.

- If the school has a business library, check to see if you can use it.

Schools may be able to help you with a specific problem. If you have a problem that would take time and knowledge to solve, try contacting a local business school. If the project is interesting, faculty members have been known to use real problems for class or group exercises.

Your local **Chamber of Commerce**. Again, these will vary in size, staff, and reference materials. Visit yours to see if and how it can help you. Besides providing reference material and suggestions, the Chamber of Commerce knows the local business environment and many important local business owners.

Trade and industry associations. Most trades and industries have an active association for their members. Your local library should have references, such as *The Encyclopedia of Associations*, published by Gale Research Company, listing all of them. Contact those associations of interest to you to see how they might be able to help you.

If there is to be a trade show of interest near you, try to attend. Most have exhibits where you will see the latest equipment and products. You can also make some excellent contacts. Warning: Admission to some shows is restricted and there may be a charge. Verify that you will be admitted before traveling to attend one. Also, be sure to have a supply of your business cards. Sometimes, your card will help to get you admitted, but your business must be in or dependent on the trade. Your card shows others that you are in business. By exchanging cards with others, you will be building your network of contacts in the industry.

Public libraries. I mention libraries several times because a good one can be a valuable source for all types of information. Most reference librarians are very competent, and can help you locate the information you need. Many libraries carry the following information:

- Demographic and economic information about your community, state, and the U.S..
- State and U.S. census information.
- A list of manufacturing companies and their product lines (The *Thomas Register of American Manufacturers* or *MacRae's Blue Book*).
- A list of almost all U.S. companies (Dun and Bradstreet).
- Financial summaries on many U.S. companies (Dun and Bradstreet).
- Business magazines.
- Business books on a variety of topics, including starting your own business.

Other sources for help

Your lawyer and accountant. You might be able to get some general information from your lawyer or accountant without charge. But remember, they make their money by providing specific knowledge and guidance. If you need their help, expect to pay for it.

Your banker and insurance agent. These people offer services which they hope you will buy. If you are a client, you can get free advice as part of their service.

Associations for small business owners. There are a number of associations, large and small, offering a variety of services. Depending on the association, the services might include free advice, publications and newsletters, and discounts on various business services such as telephone long distance charges and medical insurance. Another benefit is the ability to meet other people looking to make it on their own. Here is a partial list of these associations. Contact any of those that you believe can help you. Most will have an annual membership fee.

American Association of Professional Consultants
9140 Ward Parkway
Kansas City, MO 64114

American Home Sewing Association
1375 Broadway
New York, NY 10018

Association of Collegiate Entrepreneurs
1845 N. Fairmont
Wichita State University
Wichita, KS 67208

Association of Desktop Publishers
Box 881667
San Diego, CA 92108

The Crafts Center
2001 O Street, NW
Washington, DC 20005

Mothers Home Business Network
P.O. Box 423
East Meadow, NY 11554

National Association of the Cottage Industry
P.O. Box 1446
Chicago, IL 60614

National Association of the Self-Employed
P.O. Box 612067
DFW Airport, TX 75261

National Association of Women Business Owners
600 S. Federal Street
Chicago, IL 60605

There is only one way to make a great deal of money...and that is one's own business...but you should not start until you have acquired a good, solid working knowledge of the business - J. Paul Getty

There is no use whatever trying to help people who do not help themselves. You cannot push anyone up a ladder unless he is willing to climb himself - Andrew Carnegie

15 Why we need to be specific

As you get further into this book, you will see that I am forever encouraging you to describe things in as much detail as possible. Most of us would rather not get bogged down in detail, but in the business world, it is an important factor. Let me explain why.

We can compare starting and running a business to publishing a newspaper. We base the newspaper's reputation on the timeliness, accuracy, and thoroughness of its news stories. A good newspaper expects its reporters to cover the most important facts early in the news story. The facts are uncovered by asking a series of questions: What happened? Who was involved? Where, When, How and Why did they do it? If all these questions are answered, reporters know they have a complete story. Likewise, a business should collect all the information possible to create the complete story about itself and its market opportunity.

Why detail is important

Let's take a simple example of the importance of detail. Suppose someone asked you what business you were in, and you said, "I sell toys." That may be a good enough answer for polite conversation, but it is not adequate in business. The answer would mean too many things to different people. Now, suppose you said, "I sell high-quality, wooden, educational toys that sell for $25 to $40 for children 2 to 4 years old." Now we have some specifics. We have reduced the huge world of toys—electronic toys, dolls, games, bicycles, construction sets, hobby horses, and on-and-on—down to wooden toys. We also have eliminated cheap toys, as well as those for babies and older children.

If you are selling an expensive toy, what does that tell you about who might buy one of your toys? Certainly the child is too young to make the purchase. However, the child's parents or grandparents could, especially if they are "well-off." So to sell your toys, you should concentrate on reaching that type of parent and grandparent with your advertising.

We can go through the same exercise to describe a number of other business factors. In just about every case you can think of, more detail is better than less.

The beginning of wisdom is the definition of terms - Socrates

16 Knowing about your customers

Most large companies spend a great deal of time and money trying to understand everything they can about their customers—the people who buy their products. The companies use this information to help make decisions on product selection and pricing, advertising, selling approaches, and even how their sales people should dress and act.

Depending on the type of Mini-biz you select, it could be just as important for you to know about your customers. Since you are working on your own, let's use a simplified approach, eliminating the language the pros use, such as "market segmentation" and "target audiences."

Who are your customers?

Since customers are people, they come in all ages, sizes, education levels, income brackets, and so on. They also have different needs and interests. Depending on your Mini-biz, you may need to narrow this huge group down to the smaller group of people who will most likely buy your products or services. You will then be in a better position to use your time and money to reach those customers who can give you the most business. For example, there are dozens of ways you can advertise and sell your products or services. Knowing about your customers will help you to choose the best approaches to use.

To understand who your customers are, you need to follow two steps:

- First, you must decide on the category of people who will be your customers.

- Then you must determine who your typical customers are within that category.

Customer categories

Many small businesses have trouble defining their customers because they are confused about who their real customers are. Let's keep it simple by using two categories for you to choose from.

- You can sell directly to people (or businesses) who use your product or service themselves, or give them to other people to use (such as parents buying food, clothing, or toys for their children). The people or businesses who actually buy from you are your customers.

- You can sell to a "middleman" (for example, a retail store), who then resells your product to someone else. The retail store owner is your customer (the store owner's customer is the person who buys your product in the store).

Select the category that is appropriate for your Mini-biz. In some cases, you may be selling to both of them.

You should understand your customers' category because that is where you should be spending your advertising and selling efforts. We are used to seeing the big consumer product companies advertise to the consumer, not to the wholesaler and retailers who are their true customers (of course, they do that too--we just don't see it). On Saturday morning TV, they will advertise to small children who cannot buy, but do influence their parent's buying decisions. In both cases, the big companies are building "demand" for their products. With your Mini-biz and its limited resources, you will have to put all your efforts into reaching your customers—the people who actually buy from you.

Defining your typical customers

By now, you should have decided on the category of your customers. Let's move on to the next important step—defining your typical customers within that category. Your Mini-biz will be selling to many different types of people. However, there are one or two groups of people that best fit the description of your typical customers—those who naturally come to mind when you think about who your customers are.

Try this. Imagine yourself selling your product or service. Now think about the type of people who would most likely buy from you. These people would be your typical customers, the ones who you will concentrate on reaching with your advertising and selling effort. For example, if you are selling cosmetics directly to consumers, *females from age 14 and up* could be your customers. The cosmetics you are selling might further suggest specific age groups or income levels of females. If you are selling expensive art, *upper income married couples* will tend to be your customers. If you are selling posters of rock-and-roll stars, *teenagers and college students* might be your typical customers.

You can do the same kind of evaluation if you sell to middlemen. You should know if you are selling to retailers, wholesalers, restaurants, etc. Then, if there is something unique about those groups, you should identify it. For example, there are hundreds of different types of retailers. Your typical customers might be gift shops, or florists, or gourmet food shops, or any other special type of retailer.

Exercise

The exercise on the following page is designed to help you focus on your typical customers. Use a pencil so that you can make changes.

* **If you sell directly to the person or business** that uses your product or service, or gives them to someone else to use, fill out the top part of the form.

You will see a list of traits that might be used to describe your typical customer. In the left column, check only those traits that are important to describe your typical customers. For any traits you check, try to provide a more detailed description to the right of the check.

For example, using the example of cosmetics for 12 to 15 year old girls, you would check "Sex" in the left column, then "Female" to the right. You should also check "Age" in the left column, and "Teenager" to the right. If the cosmetics are expensive, you might want to check "Income" in the left column, and "High" to the right.

* **If you sell to middlemen**, fill out the bottom part of the form. In the left column, check off the type of middlemen you intend to sell to. To the right, describe the middlemen's businesses. For example, if you checked retailers, you might add "jewelry and gift shops" to the right.

Get the idea?

Exercise 4: Knowing about your customers

*** Fill out this part if you are selling directly to people or businesses that will use your products or services themselves (or will give—not sell—them to someone else).**

Check only <u>if important</u> **<u>Further important details</u>**

☐ Marital status: ☐Single ☐Married ☐Divorced ☐Widowed

☐ Have children ______________________________

☐ Sex: ☐Male ☐Female

☐ Age: ☐Child ☐Teenager ☐20-30 ☐31-45 ☐46-65 ☐Over 65

☐ Ethnic background ______________________________

☐ Education: ☐K-8 ☐High Sch ☐College ☐Grad school

☐ Profession ______________________________

☐ Income: ☐Low ☐Average ☐High

☐ Handicapped ______________________________

☐ Homeowner ______________________________

☐ Pet owner ______________________________

☐ Business ______________________________

☐ Other ______________________________

*** Fill out this part if your customers are "middlemen" who then sell to someone else:**

<u>Your customers could be:</u> **<u>Further important details</u>**

☐ Independent sales people ______________________________

☐ Retailers ______________________________

☐ Wholesalers ______________________________

☐ Supermarkets ______________________________

☐ Restaurants or fast food ______________________________

☐ Hotels/motels ______________________________

☐ Government agencies ______________________________

☐ Fund raisers ______________________________

☐ Other - Specify ______________________________

If you have been able to develop a "profile" of who your typical customers are, great! We will be using this information as you proceed in the book.

At first, what you have put down may not look like much, but even a small amount of information can be helpful. For example, if you "only" could determine that your typical customers—the ones who will do most of the buying of your product or service—are 12 to 15 year old girls, you have learned a great deal. You now know that to be successful you must find ways to:

- **Advertise** to reach 12 to 15 year old girls with your message about your products.

- **Sell** to 12 to 15 year old girls. This should include where and how you intend to make the sale.

Too often, business people with a good idea assume the product will sell itself. They believe the old adage, "Invent a better mousetrap, and the world will beat a path to your door." Unfortunately, this alone simply will not work. Unless people know about your products or services and can find you, your business will probably fail. Since we do not want this to happen, read on!

Give people what they want and they will make you rich - J.C. Penny

The difference between winning and losing any contest begins long before the game starts ... and it's no secret. The winner <u>expects</u> to win—the loser just <u>hopes</u> - Will Rogers

17 What you should know about competition

Do you know who your competitors are? You should know because they are a valuable source of information for you, without their even knowing it. I have mentioned competition several times in this book. This lesson will summarize what you can learn and how to use that information.

While you are still considering a specific business, you should find out who is already in that business. Then take the time to look for clues that will indicate how well they are doing. Two basic questions you would like answered are

- How big is the opportunity? - You want to know if there is enough room for your business, too.
- What is competition doing that you can do better? - If there is an unlimited opportunity, this would not be a problem. But in most cases, there will be competition. You need to know in what way the business you are planning will be better so that people will buy from you.

Before you select a business

If it is possible, spend time observing the competition. You cannot do this for all businesses, but you can for many, depending on the type of business. Here are a few examples of what you can do. Remember, you are not trying to spy or learn secrets. You merely want to get an impression of such things as quality, pricing, and customer interest. If you call on a competitor's customers, be sure the person you are talking to understands why you are there. Lesson 18 gives ideas for questions to ask. A questionnaire will help to keep your visit business-like.

- If your competitors advertise, study their ads carefully for the messages they are sending, what they think is important, and their pricing policies.

- If you are going to sell at a craft show, visit as many as you can and observe consumer interest in the types of products you intend to offer. Check prices and quality.

- If you want to do home repairs, visit homes that have had repairs. Ask if you can see the work that was performed and ask your questions.

- If you plan to offer a service to businesses, visit some with a questionnaire. You can outline your business and ask what they would like to see improved over what competition offers.

- If you plan to sell to stores, visit some and examine competitive merchandise. Observe customer reaction to the products being sold.

- You can visit other locations or towns and talk directly with people who would be your competitors if they were in your area. Since you will not be competing with them, some will be very willing to talk with you. (Then again, some may not be so willing! Do not get discouraged. Move on to the next person.)

When you have selected a business

Generally, the more you know about a business, the more likely you are to succeed. Knowing something about your competition will tell you about the business as well as what you have to do to compete. Some of the key factors you would like to know about your competitors are:

Customers

- The type of customers they attract.

- The number of customers they attract.

Products or services

- The quality of their products or services.
- How they price their products or services.
- What special services they provide.
- How they advertise.

From the list about products or services, you should ask yourself what you can do better. You should emphasize these factors in your advertising.

You should also identify those things that the competitor can do better than you can. Be honest with yourself. Are these factors important? If they are, can you "sell around" them?

Quick Tips

✓ Keeping track of your competition should be an on-going part of your business activity.

✓ Be prepared to make adjustments to your business should competition start to take customers from you.

You can succeed at almost anything for which you have unlimited enthusiasm - Charles Schwab

For of all sad words of tongue and pen,
The saddest of these: "It might have been." - John Greenleaf Whittier

18 Zero budget market research

Here is a problem. You know what kind of business you would like to start but you have no idea if it will be successful. Far too many small businesses have been started this way, on a wing and a prayer. Some businesses have been started with the notion that hard work alone will make the business go. Don't count on it.

If I suggest that what you need is some market research, you may get a little nervous. Market research can be a very expensive proposition. Large corporations spend millions of dollars and use the most advanced survey and marketing techniques, statistical programs, and computers before introducing a major new product. Even then, more new products fail than succeed in the marketplace. So what chance do you have, especially with your penny budget? The answer is that you cannot know for sure, but you can learn certain things that will help you. After all, if the big corporations continue to spend great sums of money on market research, they must see genuine value to the process. Let's see what you need to know about a new business, then determine how we can get answers.

What you can get from your market research

We know that your research cannot be perfect, but it can still provide you with some very valuable information.

- You can collect basic information about your market area and the type of people that live there. You can learn about businesses in the area.

- You can verify that some of your opinions and assumptions are correct. For example, you "just know" your product will be a winner. But do the people who might buy—your future customers—agree? Would they be willing to pay the price you will be asking? Market research can give important clues before you commit to a business.

Conducting your market research

This will take time, but it can be fun and informative. Remember what I said earlier: Spend time, not money. There are three types of research you can conduct on your own or with the help of family members: library research, observation, and interview surveys.

Library research. If you are going to operate your business locally, your library has publications from the U.S. Bureau of Census that can help. You can get information on the size and make-up of your market. This includes information on population by age and sex, ethnic background, persons per household, family income, the number of homeowners and home values, and the number of cars per household. This type of information is available at both the national and local levels, so that you can compare the two. You can also compare two adjoining localities to determine which might be better for your business.

Look for the following publications from the U.S. Department of Commerce, Bureau of Census:

Measuring Markets: A Guide to the Use of Federal and State Statistical Data. Helps you to find the specific publications with market information for the area that interests you.

Census of Population and Housing. Provides the type of information I described above for the U.S. population. *Standard Metropolitan Statistical Areas (SMSA) Reports* provide the same type of information for cities, their suburbs, and counties. *Census Tract Reports* cover the same information for some smaller sections within SMSAs.

County Business Patterns - Provides summary information on businesses by state, and counties within a state. Information is provided by business type, number and size of businesses, and number of employees.

In addition to the U.S. Census publications, your state and local governments may have their own. To find out what might be available, ask at your library or your state or local Department of Commerce, or contact your local Chamber of Commerce.

Observation. Several times in this book I have advised you to keep your eyes open, and here I am urging you again. Spend time in the area in which you intend to conduct business. Visit the area several times at different times of the day, week, and year. Look for clues that will help you to decide if you have a winning opportunity. Keep in mind that you are like a reporter. You have your best answers to the "Who, What...." questions asked earlier, and now you want to verify those facts. Since the range of opportunities is endless, there is no way that I can give you an exact list of things to watch for. However, I can give some examples.

- How are people (your potential customers) dressed? What type of vehicle do they drive? Do many of them match your answer to the question "Who will buy your product or service?"

- Watch your competition. Are they busy? What type of customer patronizes them? Are they the same type of customer you expect? What can you do better then the competition? How much do they charge? Is there enough business if you move in, too?

- If you plan to offer a home repair or house painting service, look through the neighborhoods you plan to service. Are there homes in need of repair? The outside appearance may give you clues to the condition of the inside.

Interview surveys. There are many ways to conduct surveys, including by telephone, by mail, or through group interviews (focus groups). Most of these techniques are too expensive for a Mini-biz. However, you can still conduct personal interviews to collect opinions and some valuable information and ideas. There are important limits that you must remember.

- Do not expect absolute answers. Use the survey results with caution to give you some idea of how your business might fare. The accuracy of any survey depends on a number of factors, including quality of the survey questions, how the survey is administered, the number of participants, and data-reduction techniques. In a large company, these factors would be addressed by experts. Even then, they would state a "margin of error" that reflects their confidence in the accuracy of their results.

- You need to interview those who represent the type of people who make the "buying decision" for your product or service. If you know your typical customer will be a middle-aged woman, then interview middle-aged women. If you are not sure of your customer type, you may want to interview two or three types.

- Do not confuse the person who will use your product or service with the person who makes the buying decision (the person you want to interview). For example, in the toy business I mentioned earlier, you may want to get the reaction of a child (to see if he or she likes it). However, you certainly want to get the reaction of parents and grandparents regarding price and buying interest.

- Avoid family and friends as part of your sample. They will want the best for you and will tend to be too positive. However, feel free to talk to them about ways to improve your business.

Conducting interviews requires preparation.

1. Decide what information you want to collect. Let's say you have a specific product in mind (for example, a toy) and want to know if you can sell enough to start your Mini-biz. You also want to know if the price you intend to charge is acceptable.

2. Prepare a list of questions you want answered. Limit the number of questions, and keep them short and simple. Prepare two types of questions:

   - Questions about the person you are interviewing. Only ask questions that relate to your business needs. For example, do you have children? How old are they? ... Do <u>not</u> get too personal or ask embarrassing questions.

   - Questions about your product or service. Try to prepare questions with yes or no answers. Another popular technique is to solicit answers on a scale from 1 (for very positive) to 5 (for very negative). A neutral answer or no opinion would then be 3. These types of answers are easy to record during the interview and easy to summarize later.

3. Prepare and practice a short script so that you can approach people to ask them if they will respond to your survey. For a toy product, you might say something like this:

"Excuse me, sir (ma'am) .... I am not selling anything, but I am conducting a survey to get people's opinions on a new product (or service) that I am planning to offer. I would really value your opinions. May I have just a few minutes of your time?

Thank you.

Do you live in this area? How often do you shop at this mall? Do you have any children? What are there ages? Now, I would like to show you a product (or picture of a product) to get your reaction. As you can see it is very attractive and extremely durable. Besides, it is ... (list major features). Can I ask what you think of the product? Please answer on a scale of 1 to 5, 1 being very positive, and 5 being very negative, and 3 being neutral:

- What do you think of the product?
- Do you think children you know would like it?
- Do you know a child for whom you would consider buying it?
- Would you pay $29.95 for it?

  If not, what would you pay?

Thank you very much for your time and honest opinions. You have been very helpful. Have a nice day."

Do you get the idea?

4. Prepare a worksheet. You will need one for each person you interview. At the top, list some things you want to observe and note about the person without asking, such as sex and approximate age. Then list the questions you want to ask, leaving space for you to write. When the survey is ready, get copies made at a local copy center.

5. You are now able to start interviewing. You can try this approach at malls, door-to-door, at flea markets, or with businesses. Warning: At a privately operated facility, such as a mall, you would be wise to get the approval of its managers before you start. Dress neatly and approach people with a smile to put them at ease. One touch that will make you look very

businesslike is to carry and work from a clipboard. Ask your questions and encourage their comments. Take notes.

6. I recommend that you conduct as many interviews as possible. By doing this, you will see people's reaction and hear their comments first hand. You also may find it necessary to change some questions to get more accurate results. If you want more interviews than you can conduct yourself, you can use family members or qualified housewives or college students.

7. If you will be selling to businesses, your approach may be different. You should arrange to meet with the person who makes the buying decision. Start the meeting by saying you are doing some research to decide if you will commit to your Mini-biz. Then give the "sales pitch" you would use if you were actually selling. Ask if he or she would buy your product or services. If the answer is no, try to get the reasons why not. Also ask what it would take to get their business. Finally, if you are selling products where many units would be bought, ask how many units the potential customer would use per month or year.

The secret of business is to know something that nobody else knows - Aristotle Onassis

19 A "business plan" for your Mini-biz

While a business plan is essential when starting a typical company, you do not need a full plan for a Mini-biz. However, you will need something. Let's start by describing what a business plan is.

A business plan can be compared to both a blueprint and a road map. It describes a company in great detail, covering management, products, production, marketing, revenue and profit projections, etc. It shows where your company is now, where you want to go, what has to be done to get there, and how much money is needed along the way. If the company needs to borrow money, lenders will want to review the plan in detail. Not only can lenders judge how good the plan is, but they can also judge management's ability to run the company. For these reasons, preparing a business plan can be a very time-consuming and expensive project. Depending on the complexity and financial needs of the company, plans normally run from ten to over 100 pages of detailed information.

Many of the important areas that would be part of a business plan are covered in this book. There are two critical areas where you should spend some time answering questions about your Mini-biz: finance and marketing. The following exercises are designed to help you determine if you are headed in the right direction.

Exercise 5 deals with your financial needs. It covers both your initial expenses and your operating expenses.

Exercise 6 asks important questions about your marketing plans.

Exercise 5 | Looking at your financial needs

Initial Expenses

Depending on the Mini-biz you select, you may have startup expenses. I have listed some typical ones here. Check all those that apply to your Mini-biz, and estimate what each will cost. Use a pencil so that you can make changes.

Needed	Estimated
☐ Training or manuals	$ ______
☐ Fees paid to other companies	$ ______
☐ Inventory	$ ______
☐ Tools or equipment	$ ______
☐ Office equipment	$ ______
☐ Supplies and stationary	$ ______
☐ Attorney fees	$ ______
☐ Business insurance	$ ______
☐ Licenses or permits	$ ______
☐ Early advertising	$ ______
☐ Other ________________	$ ______
________________	$ ______
________________	$ ______
TOTAL	$ ______

Can you afford this?

☐ Yes (required answer)

☐ No. If no, you should either look for a different Mini-biz, or work on ways to get the required money.

Exercise 5

Operating expenses: budgets and cash flow

Operating expenses are those incurred to operate the business during a period of time. They will vary depending on the type of Mini-biz. To understand these expenses, we have two accounting tools, a budget and a cash-flow analysis. Although budgets and cash flow are critical concerns to most businesses, large or small, they may or may not be important at the start of yours.

Quiz

Answer the following questions as best you can. Your answers will help to determine what you need to do.

1. Will you have to spend much money to get started? (Such as paying for inventory, a special course, or special equipment)
   ☐Yes ☐No ☐Don't know

2. Will your business have any big fixed monthly costs? (Such as rent, salaries, telephone and utility bills)
   ☐Yes ☐No ☐Don't know

3. Will you have to wait a long time before you start to see customers?
   ☐Yes ☐No ☐Don't know

4. After a sale, will you have to wait a long time to get paid by customers?
   ☐Yes ☐No ☐Don't know

5. If your answer is "Yes" or "Don't know" to <u>any</u> of questions 1 to 4, would you have trouble taking care of your usual personal and family expenses?
   ☐Yes ☐No ☐Don't know

What to do next

If you answered "No" to all five questions, a simple budget like the one on the next page is all you will have to prepare.

If your answer to question 5 is "Yes" or "Don't know," you need to do the simplified cash-flow analysis on page 85.

Exercise 5

Instructions for budget exercise on opposite page

GETTING STARTED: Decide which 6-month period you want to examine. All estimates you make should be for the full 6-month period.

1. INCOME: Estimate the income you will be making from sales of your products or services for the 6-month period.

2. EXPENSES: List the expenses you will have and estimate how much you will spend for each expense. Add them and enter the amount on the Total Expenses line. The amount shown in the example is more than the $1000 limit set for a Mini-biz. Keep in mind that you are estimating your expenses for a 6-month period. I assume you will be selling your products during that period and you will be putting some of your profits back into the business. Your initial investment could be well below $1000. To start, you would have paid the $300 for equipment but only a portion of the supplies and advertising expenses.

3. PROJECTED GROSS PROFIT (OR LOSS): Subtract the Total Expenses (item 2) from Income (item 1). If the result is a negative number, it indicates a loss.

4. CONTINGENCY: Because you are estimating about the future, you will not know the real numbers. You should add a contingency amount to allow for estimating errors and omissions. I used a 25% contingency because I assumed the owner of the XYZ Company was somewhat uncomfortable with his estimates. You can use a larger or smaller percentage depending on how good you think your estimates are. Remember: better to be safe than sorry.

5. PROFIT/LOSS MINUS CONTINGENCY: Subtracting Line 4 from Line 3 will give you your estimated profit or loss for the 6-month period. The example of the XYZ Company is used only to illustrate how to estimate your budget. Your profits could be less, or a great deal more, depending on your Mini-biz. The bigger the positive number, the better! A very small number means you are not making enough money for the time and money you are investing. A negative number means you are losing money! Check your figures. If things still look unsatisfactory, consider a different Mini-biz.

Exercise 5

Budgets

A budget is an itemized list of expenses and income for a period of time. Below, is a simplified budget for the "XYZ Widget Company." To the right, there is space for you to try a budget for your Mini-biz. Use a pencil so that you can make changes.

		Example		*Your Budget*
		XYZ Widget Company		________
		For the 6 Month Period January through June		For the 6 month Period ____ through ____
1. PROJECTED INCOME				
Product sales		$10,000		$ ____
2. PROJECTED EXPENSES				
Equipment	$300		$ ____	
Supplies	800		____	
Advertising	500		____	
____________	--		____	
____________	--		____	
____________	--		____	
TOTAL EXPENSES		1,600		____
3. PROJECTED PROFIT OR LOSS (if -)		8,400		____
4. CONTINGENCY	(25%)	2,100	(___%)	____
5. PROFIT/LOSS LESS CONTINGENCY		$6,300		$ ____

Exercise 5

Instructions for cash-flow exercise on opposite page

To be safe, be conservative whenever you estimate. Remember, even the biggest companies are often off when they forecast the future of new products. By being conservative, you are helping to protect your business.

1. CASH ON HAND: Start on Line 1 for Month 1. Write in the amount of money you intend to put into your Mini-biz. When you have estimated down through Line 7 for Month 1, copy that number onto Line 1 of Month 2.

2. MONTHLY INCOME: You have to estimate what your dollar sales will be (the big guys call this "forecasting"). There are several ways you can approach this. You can estimate how many widgets you will sell, then multiply this by the average selling price. If you are selling a service, you can estimate how many jobs you think you will get and the average price per job.

3. TOTAL CASH: Add the amounts in Steps 1 and 2 to get the total amount of money you will have before paying your expenses.

4. FIXED COSTS: List those costs that occur every month regardless of sales (for example, rent, insurance, some utilities, and any salaries you might be paying).

5. VARIABLE COSTS: List those costs that change depending on how much you buy or sell each month. For example, the cost of goods you purchase and the commissions you pay on sales.

6. TOTAL MONTHLY COSTS: Add the amounts in Steps 4 and 5 to get your total expenses for the month.

7. CASH BALANCE: Subtract the amounts shown in Step 6 from those in Step 3. This is the estimated amount of money you will have at the end of each month. The bigger the better! On the other hand, a negative cash balance indicates that you will be <u>short of funds</u> for that month. Do you know how you will cover expenses? That is, do you know where you can get the money to pay your bills to keep going? If yes, fine. If not, double check your estimates. If they seem to be as accurate as you can estimate, you better think again before moving ahead on this venture.

Exercise 5

Cash-flow analysis

A cash-flow analysis shows the flow of money into and out of a business. It helps you to project when your business will receive money and when it must spend money to pay bills. From this you will be able to judge when the business will have extra money and when it will need more. A cash-flow analysis can get very complex. However, you will have a limited number of expenses when starting a Mini-biz. This will help to simplify your analysis.

Your simplified cash-flow projections

MONTH	1	2	3	4	5	6
1. CASH ON HAND (Start of month)	_____	_____	_____	_____	_____	_____
2. MONTHLY INCOME	_____	_____	_____	_____	_____	_____
3. TOTAL CASH (Add 1 and 2)	_____	_____	_____	_____	_____	_____
4. FIXED COSTS						
______________________	_____	_____	_____	_____	_____	_____
______________________	_____	_____	_____	_____	_____	_____
______________________	_____	_____	_____	_____	_____	_____
5. VARIABLE COSTS						
______________________	_____	_____	_____	_____	_____	_____
______________________	_____	_____	_____	_____	_____	_____
______________________	_____	_____	_____	_____	_____	_____
6. TOTAL MONTHLY COSTS (Add 4 and 5)	_____	_____	_____	_____	_____	_____
7. CASH BALANCE (Subtract 6 from 3)	_____	_____	_____	_____	_____	_____

Exercise 5

Estimating the amount of money you can make

Estimating how much money you could make from a business is a difficult task because of the many factors that must be considered. These include:

- The amount of time and effort you will put into the business.
- Your ability to do the job. Some of us are better salespersons than others, some are more creative, others more efficient, and so on.
- The quality and value of your products or services.
- The number of competitors and the quality of their products or services.
- The "market potential" for your business. That is, how many potential customers there are who would be willing and able to buy your product or service.

With this number of variables, there is no formula that will generate a number that projects how well you will do in a specific business. On the other hand, you can get some ideas from three sources:

- If you are working with suppliers, they can give you insight into how well others are doing financially.
- Watch your competitors (see Lesson 17).
- Conduct market research (see Lesson 18).

A problem well stated is a problem half solved - Charles Kettering

Exercise 6 | Looking at your marketing needs

Every business needs some sort of marketing plan. Don't panic. It does not have to be very fancy for a Mini-biz. In a large corporation, the marketing plan for each product is very detailed and covers a wide range of activities. Some of the activities include defining the product, its "market potential," pricing, competition, and how it will be advertised, distributed, and sold. Your Mini-biz might need to address many of these same activities. Since you are working on your own, without an army of experts, do the best you can using the simplified approach of this exercise. Use a pencil so that you can make changes.

Before you start your business, you should know:

1. **Who are your customers?** This was covered in Lesson 16.

2. **Who are your competitors?** (Lesson 17). List your main ones:

 ____

 ____

3. **Why will your customers buy from you?** That is, what features and advantages do you offer over competition? For example, better price, quality, reliability, design, service, etc.

 ____

 ____

4. **How many customers might buy from you?** That is, do you believe there are enough potential customers that will buy from you?

 ☐ Yes (preferred answer) ☐ Probably (may be acceptable) ☐ No

 If yes or probably, what reasons can you give for this opinion?

 ____

 ____

 ____

Exercise 6

5. **How and where will you sell?** Every business requires selling. List the way(s) you intend to use. If you are not sure, Lesson 32 gives many suggestions. ____

____

____

6. **When will you sell?** If the business is seasonal, or only effective during certain hours or days, list here. ______________________________

____

____

7. **How and when will you advertise and publicize your business?** Somehow, you must let people know about your business. Lessons 33 to 35 discuss many ways you can advertise and publicize your products or services. Briefly list your plans here:

Advertising

____

____

____

Publicity

____

____

____

To improve your chances for success, you should be able to fill in something in each category <u>before</u> you start the business. If you have any doubts about where you stand, do your homework now. It can save you many frustrating hours and a great deal of money later on. For example, if you do not know how to reach your intended customers, how do you expect them to learn about your business? Or, if you intend to advertise, do you have the necessary money?

Section F
Getting Ready

In the ordinary business of life, industry can do anything which genius can do, and very many things which it cannot - Harriet Ward Beecher

20 How important is location?

You probably have heard it said that the three most important factors for a business are location, location, and location. I believe this statement can do more harm than good. Owners of new businesses may place too much emphasis on location, and not enough on the rest of their business needs. Certainly location is critical for some businesses. But the best location in the world will not help you to sell an unacceptable product or service. Nor will taking in buckets of money guarantee your business will be profitable.

A more realistic statement would be, "For some businesses, location is <u>one of several</u> key factors." For retail businesses, a good location is one with heavy traffic that can easily be visited by customers. However, many retailers cannot afford to pay the higher rents that may be charged for these prime places. As someone trying to start with a small budget, you probably do not have a choice. That's okay. Just understand your options so that you can get around this limitation:

- You can select a business that will allow you operate from your home or garage, with customers and clients coming to you. Before committing to a home business, check your local zoning codes (see Lesson 24).

  If you live in a rural area, make sure that there are enough local customers who will come to you, or that more distant ones will be willing to make the trip. Businesses that have succeeded this way include produce stands, rock and hobby shops, carpentry shops, antique shops, and kennels.

- You can consider businesses with no direct customer contact, such as mail order or a telephone answering service. Again, check zoning codes.

- You can go to the customer's home or business place. This can take many forms. For example:

  Door-to-door sales.

  Home party plans.

  Visiting in response to an inquiry.

  Making repairs and improvements to customers' offices, homes, or yards.

  Selling to stores and other businesses.

- You may be able to find office or storage space in an established business that you can rent at a reduced rate. If you have a product or service that the other business can use, you may be able to barter (exchange) your offerings for space. The same approaches can be tried to get counter space in a store.

- In many cities, you can find offices that offer a variety of business services including office space, a mailing address, secretarial services, and fax and copier usage. Since several people share the facility, rents are reasonable. Check in your telephone classified under "Office and desk space rental."

- You can rent space at fairs and flea markets where rent is usually very reasonable. Some shopping malls will also rent you space in the common areas between stores.

- If you are adventurous and have the right product, there are always street corners, parking lots, and road shoulders near stop signs where you can set up and sell. You might have to forget this one in cities and towns with ordinances against this type of selling.

Often we look so long at the closed door that we do not see the one which has opened for us - Helen Keller

21 Selecting the legal form of your Mini-biz

Any money-making activity you operate for a period of time is considered to be a business. One of the things you will have to decide is the legal form of your Mini-biz. While there are many variations, there are four basic forms: sole proprietorships, partnerships, corporations, and sub-chapter S corporations. There are a number of factors that normally go into making a decision on which to use. For your Mini-biz, I recommend you start as a proprietorship if you are the only owner. If there is more than one owner, I recommend starting as a partnership. The following summaries will help to explain my recommendations.

Sole proprietorship

In this form, you are the sole owner of the business. This is the simplest form, and there is little paperwork involved.

Advantages

- The business is easy to set up.
- You run the show.
- All profits are yours alone.
- You can gain tax advantages. You can deduct legitimate business expenses from personal taxes.

Disadvantages

- You are personally liable for any debts or law suits against the business.
- You must make all decisions.
- Personal finances can easily get mixed with the business's.

Partnership

This business has two or more owners. It can be set up by oral agreement among the owners. However, I strongly recommend that the agreement be put in writing with a lawyer's involvement.

In some companies, partners share responsibilities, each contributing what he or she does best. In some cases, partners may not actively work in the business, but only contribute money or advice. They are known as "silent partners." There are also "limited partnerships" where a partner has a limited role in the operations of the business. There may be tax advantages, especially if family members are involved.

Advantages

- Partners can share responsibilities and expenses.
- Each partner can do what he or she does best.
- Partners can cover for each other, allowing time off.

Disadvantages

- Each partner can be held responsible for business debts or legal actions against the company.
- A partner may be held responsible for the bad actions of another partner.
- Friction can develop among partners, especially in bad times.
- Like a broken marriage, dissolving a bad partnership can be messy.

Corporation

This is more elaborate than the other forms. Almost all major companies and many other companies are incorporated. When a corporation is formed, ownership shares are sold to people, who become shareholders. In turn, they elect a board of directors, who then elect the officers who run the company. In a small, privately-owned corporation, the shareholders, directors, and officers may be the same people.

Advantages

- The corporation has a "legal entity" separate from the shareholders who own it. This may limit shareholder's liability for debts and legal actions against the corporation.
- Ownership (shares) in the company can easily be transferred.
- Growth can be easier to accomplish. You can raise money by selling additional stocks.

Disadvantages

- Corporations are more difficult and expensive to set up. You should seek a lawyer's advice.
- Profits may be taxed twice. The corporation pays taxes on profits and stockholder's pay taxes on dividends.
- A state charter is required. The corporation must conform to state and federal regulations.
- More paperwork and documentation of actions are necessary.
- For tax purposes, you will be an employee of the corporation. Therefore, most of the tax paperwork and record keeping described in Lesson 28 will have to be maintained.

Sub-Chapter S Corporation

This business form is considered a corporation in all ways except regarding taxes. It offers distinct tax advantages over other business forms, especially in the business's early days. As the company grows, you can change over to a corporation.

This is not for amateurs. If you want to know more, contact your lawyer and accountant. I suggest you skip this one for now, but keep it in mind for future consideration.

Quick Tips

✓ As I said earlier, most readers should start their businesses as sole proprietorships. Therefore, it is important to select a business where there is little likelihood that you will be held liable for product or property damage. If in doubt, check with your insurance agent and lawyer.

✓ As the business grows, you should consider forming a corporation or sub-chapter S corporation. This will usually give you better liability protection and more tax advantages.

In all things, success depends on previous preparation, and without such preparation, there is sure failure - Confucius

22 Your business bank account

To keep good records—and to maintain your sanity—I urge you to set up a separate checking account for your business. If your company's name is different from your own, having the company name on company checks will enhance your image of being in business. This is especially true when paying suppliers or if you should have to write a check payable to a customer.

In most cases, you probably should set up a business savings account as well. Properly used, a business account will help you to keep your business finances separate from your personal finances. With this, you can simplify record keeping for tax purposes and gain an accurate picture of how well your business is doing.

To make the system work, pay business expenses by check from your business account and deposit all business receipts into the account.

Quick Tips:

✓ If you see your business growing, you may want to shop around for your business bank. You will find that charges and services will vary among banks. You may also find that banks treat business accounts differently from personal accounts.

✓ As you grow, you may need to borrow from a bank. You will find some banks are more interested in helping small businesses than others. If the first banks you try turn you down, do not become discouraged. Find out why you were rejected, and develop a plan around those reasons when approaching the next bank.

Enthusiasm is the mother of effort, and without it nothing great was ever accomplished - Ralph Waldo Emerson

23 Do you need permits or licenses?

Whether you will need to register your Mini-biz to operate will depend on three factors: the state, city, or county in which you plan to work, the type of business you intend to operate, and the name you give your business.

State and local regulations

The need to have a business license or permit varies from state to state and from location to location. If you have no problems with the other requirements described in this lesson, it is possible that you will not have to register at all. However, I strongly recommend you do check with your appropriate state, county, or town agencies.

The business you intend to operate

If your state has a retail sales tax, and if you intend to sell products within your state, you will be required to collect the tax. See Lesson 26, under "State Sales Tax," for details.

If your Mini-biz is a **partnership or corporation**, registration will be required.

Some **occupations** require a license or permit, whether you work for yourself or for someone else. A test may be required, and you may have to pay a small fee.

Typical occupations that might require a license or permit in your locality include:

Auctioneers
Bakers and Cooks
Beauticians and Barbers
Business Agents
Check Cashers
Contractors
Electricians
Employment Agencies
Exterminators
Florists
Insurance agents
Landscape architects
Manufacturers
Masseurs
Mechanics
Motor vehicle salesmen
Nursery operators
Nursing home operators
Pawnbrokers
Plumbers
Real estate agents
Restaurant owners
Vending machine owners
Taxi drivers

You should check any type of food or drink preparation or handling business. Health ordinances could apply in your community.

Your company name

If you give your Mini-biz a name other than your own, you have to register that name (see Lesson 29).

Quick Tip

✓ Remember, requirements for licenses and permits vary from state to state and locality to locality. If in doubt about any of these requirements for your locality, check with the appropriate government office such as your county clerk's office. Your local Chamber of Commerce might be able to advise you.

Few things are impossible to diligence and skill - Samuel Johnson

24 What about zoning restrictions?

There are millions of people working from their homes, and the number is growing. Without knowing it, many of them may be violating local zoning restrictions that forbid any or certain types of work at home.

Zoning laws are written to specify how real estate in different areas of a city or town can be used. There may be areas or zones specified for single-family homes, or apartments, or factories, or stores. Each type of zone has restrictions put in place to protect the interests of people living or working there. For example, would you like to live in a big, expensive home and see a factory built next door? Just think of the trucks, traffic, noise, and fumes. Zoning an area as "residential only" prevents this from happening.

Unfortunately, many zoning restrictions were written years ago and may not make sense today. Certainly you still would not want a factory next door to your home. But would you mind a consultant working at a personal computer, or a commercial artist preparing layouts for clients?

If you lived in an area zoned "residential," your neighbors probably would complain if you conducted a business that caused excessive and annoying noise or traffic. If they reported you, a review of local ordinances might force you to close the business or move. On the other hand, your neighbors probably would not mind or even notice a business that did not cause any unusual activity or noise. Today there are many businesses operating from homes in violation of the <u>wording</u> of an ordinance, but not necessarily of its <u>intent.</u>

Quick Tips

If you plan to work from your home:

✓ Always be a good neighbor. Consider others' rights and desire to live in a pleasant neighborhood. Not only is this fair, but it makes good business sense.

✓ Check with your local zoning office or look for a copy of local zoning regulations at your public library. Regulations vary from town to town. Check to see if your planned business would be in violation.

✓ If you anticipate your business will be in violation, you have several courses of action:

- If you meet the intent, take a chance and proceed. You may never have a problem. Then again, you may. You will have to assess the risk for your business in your community.
- You can select a different business opportunity that would not be in violation.
- You can appeal to the zoning board for special permission to operate your business if you believe you meet the intent of the ordinance AND you are not causing disruptions in the neighborhood.
- You can appeal to the zoning board for a change in the ordinance. You may be able to get support from others in the neighborhood who are interested in starting their own home businesses.

Everything is funny as long as it happens to somebody else -
Will Rogers

25 Does your business need insurance?

Insurance is an item that is often overlooked by the small business owner. Be aware that standard home or vehicle insurance may not cover business activities. However, in many cases you can get business insurance added to your standard policy at low cost.

As with all insurance, the critical factors that determine cost are the likelihood of a problem and what it costs to fix it or compensate you.

For example, if you are an author writing at home there should be little if any difference in your insurance premium. If you buy an expensive computer and printer, you would then want to make sure that they were covered by your home policy.

Now take the case where you are making and storing a large number of wooden toys in your basement. You are also storing containers of volatile paint used to decorate the toys. No matter how safely you work, in this case it is likely that you will need extra insurance protection for the business.

Key areas you should review for insurance

Your home. If you have:

- Business visitors coming to your home.
- People working in your home.
- Expensive business equipment.
- Potentially hazardous activities or materials.

Your car or truck. If it is used for business purposes.

Products you sell. If they could cause possible harm.

Services you perform. If they could leave a hazardous condition (example, slippery floors) or liability (example, financial losses from bad advice).

Quick Tips

✓ Consider what possible risks your business might have. Remember, today you can be sued for almost any reason.

✓ Review your home and vehicle policies and discuss them with your insurance agent.

✓ Tell your agent if you are using your home or possessions for the business. Not telling him could make it difficult for you to collect if you file an insurance claim.

✓ Premiums you pay for insurance for the business are tax deductible.

✓ If you hire people, remember you can be held responsible for their actions on the job.

✓ As your business grows, review your health and life insurance. A key question: What would happen if you could not run the business?

One does not trip over mountains, but over molehills - Confucius

26 What about taxes?

Hey...Read this!

Of all the lessons in the book, this is the one most people would like to skip. Taxes suggest two painful situations: frustrating paperwork and taking hard-earned money out of our pockets. But please read on. It could save you a great deal of trouble—and maybe some money—in the future.

Tax laws are downright confusing. Not only are they complicated, but they are constantly changing. In addition, they vary from federal, to state, to municipality. It's enough to make a tax lawyer rich!

There is no way that I can discuss all aspects of the various taxes in this book. Instead, I will concentrate on tax basics for a sole proprietorship, the business form that most readers will be using at the start. I will also touch on some tax situations you may have to face as your company grows.

State sales tax

This tax applies to any business with retail sales. In effect, you are acting as a tax collector for the state. You collect the tax with each retail sale, then pass the money to your state's revenue department. Most states have a retail sales tax. If you live in one of these states, you should be familiar with the tax because it is added to a wide variety of purchases you make.

You must apply at your state revenue department for a selling permit. There usually is a small charge. You will have to forward tax money every month or every three months, depending on your state's rules. With the permit, you will not have to pay state taxes on products you buy to resell, or on raw materials you buy to make products to sell.

State sales taxes usually apply only to:

- Retail sales, not wholesale or service businesses.

- Sales made within the state. If you sell a product by mail order to someone outside your state, you would not collect the tax. If you ship to a customer in the state, you would.

Taxes on income and business profit

Most readers will be starting their businesses as sole proprietorships. The government will require you to report and pay taxes on any profit from the business along with your personal income tax.

Federal taxes. The minimum paperwork incudes the preparation of the following forms:

- As always, use Tax Form 1040 to report your income. Income includes salary from other jobs, stock dividends, interest income, etc., etc.

- Use Form 1040, Schedule C to report profit (or loss) from your business. You also list all business deductions.

- Use Form 4562 if you are depreciating or amortizing any property (buildings, vehicles, machines, etc.).

- Once you are making more than $400 from your business, you will have to file Form 1040-Schedule SE, "Social Security Self-Employment Tax."

- Although all of these forms must be filed by April 15 every year, the government does not want to wait that long to be paid. You may have to estimate your taxes on income and profits and pay four times a year—by the 15th of January, April, June, and September. Use Tax Form 1040-ES for this purpose.

- If your business is a partnership, any income each partner takes from the business must be reported on his individual 1040 Tax Form. In addition, you must file Form 1065, which deals with the profit (or loss) and operation of the business.

State taxes. Many states have income and business profits taxes. Many are patterned after federal laws, but there could be differences in procedures and rates. Check with your state revenue department.

Municipal taxes. If your city has an income tax, you probably will have to report your business activities. Check with your municipal revenue department.

Quick Tips

✓ Unless your business is extremely simple and small, I recommend you seek help in tax planning and the preparation of tax returns. You want to "stay clean" with the tax authorities. You want to avoid hassles and audits so that you can concentrate on growing your business. You also want to take the maximum business deductions to which you are entitled.

✓ With the explosion of interest in small businesses, there are many accountants and tax preparers who are well-versed in small business tax matters. Interview several to find one you can afford and who understands your needs.

✓ Even with a good accountant or tax expert, you should spend time learning tax basics. The federal Internal Revenue Service has many free publications that can help you. Here is a list of "kits" containing several publications:

Free IRS publications

Kit Number	Title
YBTK-S	Your Business Tax Kit - Sole Proprietorship
YBTK-P	Your Business Tax Kit - Partnership
YBTK-C	Your Business Tax Kit - Corporation

Each "YBTK" kit contains a number of publications, including those with * on the next page.

Publication Number	Title
15*	Employer's Tax Guide (Circular E)
17	Your Federal Income Tax
334*	Tax Guide for Small Business
463	Travel, Entertainment, and Business Expenses
505*	Tax Withholding and Estimated Taxes
508	Educational Expenses
509*	Tax Calendar
533*	Self-Employment Tax
534	Depreciation
535	Business Expenses
539*	Employment Taxes
541	Tax Information on Partnerships
552	Recordkeeping for Individuals
553	Highlight of Year Tax Changes
560	Self-Employed Retirement Plans
583*	Information for Business Taxpayers
587	Business Use of Your Home
590	IRAs
850	Glossary of Terms
910*	Guide to Free Tax Services
911	Tax Information for Direct Sellers
917	Business Use of Your Car
926	Employment Taxes for Household Employers

* These publications are included in the "YBTK" kits shown on the previous page.

Some of these publications are available at your local IRS office. Or you may order them by telephone through 1-800-829-3676 (1-800-TAX-FORM).

The hardest thing in the world to understand is the income tax -
Albert Einstein

27 Tax deductions: the good tax news

In the last lesson, I discussed your tax obligations. Now let's talk about the good news—the business deductions you can take which will ease your tax burden. A word of caution. As with many tax rules, those regarding deductions are subject to change, and are more than I can cover in this book. Therefore, this is a general discussion to provide some understanding. I will concentrate on those factors that are most likely to affect you. As your business grows, I urge you to work with an accountant or tax preparer who is familiar with small businesses. IRS publication 535 provides a good overview of many business expenses.

Normal business deductions

Many expenses in the day-to-day operation of business are legitimate tax deductions. Here are <u>some</u> examples:

Business rent
Business insurance
Utilities
Interest charges on business loans
Stationery and office supplies
License and permit fees
Business books and magazine subscriptions
Professional fees—lawyers, accountants, consultants
Business meals, entertainment, and travel
Association fees
Education for business purposes
Work clothes
Salaries to employees

Bad debts
Tax advice and preparation expenses

The IRS may take a close look at the deductions you claim. To minimize problems, ask yourself three questions. Is the deduction

1. Truly related to the business?

2. "Ordinary and necessary"—is it appropriate and needed to run your business?

3. Reasonable in cost?

IRS Publication 529 has more information on miscellaneous deductions.

Special situations

Using your home for business. Many readers will be in this category, at least as they start their business. Over the years, the IRS has tended to tighten these rules. Currently, they allow deductions only for that part of your house that is used "regularly and exclusively" as

- Your principal place of business.

- A place to meet with clients or customers in the normal course of your business.

In other words, you can only deduct those portions of your home that are used exclusively for your business. For example, it cannot also be used as a den or family room. If you can identify such an area, calculate its size in square feet. Then divide that area by the total square feet for your house. This will give you the percentage of your house expenses you may be able to deduct from your business, depending on whether it made or lost money that year. Typical expenses could include rent, utilities, insurance, and taxes.

IRS publication 587 has more information on deductions when you use your home for business use.

Depreciation. You may have to purchase some rather expensive equipment for your business—a machine, or personal computer, or specialized tools, for example. If the equipment has a useful life of over one year, you can claim a tax deduction for a portion of its cost for several years. The "depreciation" or "write off" period the IRS will allow varies by the type of equipment. Time periods are three years or longer. There are several ways that depreciation can be handled, so you should consult a tax expert to get the maximum benefit allowed.

There is another method of treating this type of equipment. You can deduct up to $10,000 of equipment purchases made in one year. As with most tax matters, there are a number of restrictions. For example, you cannot deduct a larger amount than the profit your business makes in the same year. Again, if you have questions, you should contact your tax expert.

If you would like to learn more, IRS publication 534 provides a great deal of detail.

Vehicle use and expenses. If you own a car, van or truck, I assume you could be using it for your new business. You can deduct vehicle expenses related to the business portion of the vehicle's use. Although there is more than one way to calculate this, the simplest way is to keep track of miles traveled for business purposes. Keep a log showing date and mileage. The IRS will allow you to take a deduction based on the "standard mileage rate." Currently, this rate is 27½ cents per mile.

IRS publication 917 has more on using your car for business.

Cost of goods sold. If you make or buy products to sell, you can deduct the "cost of goods sold." Depending on your business, these costs can be quite complicated to calculate. This is especially true if you are making products using many raw materials, or if your business grows in size and complexity.

Let's take a simple example to understand the concept. In your business you buy and sell widgets. Your first year, you start with no widgets. During the year you purchase a total of $5,000 worth of widgets. (This is your cost to buy them, not your selling price). At the end of the year, you take inventory and calculate the value of the widgets you still have in stock. Let's say they are worth $1,000 (once again, based on your cost). Subtracting $1,000 from $5,000 leaves $4,000, the cost of the widgets you sold during the year, and the amount you can deduct on your taxes.

IRS publication 334 has more detail on cost of goods sold. In fact, this publication covers many tax topics of interest to the small business owner.

Tax-deferred retirement plans: IRAs and Keogh plans

NOTE: You are probably not ready for this topic yet, but it is worth reading so that you can start thinking about the day when you will be making a significant profit. It will also illustrate one of the nice benefits to having your own business.

I do not know your age, but I will make the blanket statement, "Consider your future." Two government-sponsored programs that can help are the Keogh Plan and Individual Retirement Arrangements (IRAs). These programs have some similarities. As "tax-deferred retirement plans," they both are designed to allow you to put aside some of your income and invest it in your future. The income you put aside will not be taxed until you withdraw it. Normally, you cannot start to take money out until you are 59½ to 70½ years old without paying a penalty. You will have to pay taxes at that time, but the theory is that you will be retired with less income and therefore in a lower tax bracket. In addition, soundly invested, the money should appreciate significantly.

Keogh Plans are primarily for the self-employed, but you may have to include people working for you. There are several types of plans; the maximum you can invest is 20% of your profit, up to $30,000 each year.

IRAs are available to all employees, as well as many self-employed. You can contribute up to $2000 a year to IRAs, and if you have a non-working spouse, you can contribute a total of $2250. However, the amount you can deduct from present taxes will vary from no deduction, to partial, to full deduction. The amount that is allowed is based on a number of factors, including your tax bracket.

If you are self employed, you may be able to take advantage of both plans. If you would like to learn more, order IRS publications 560 and 590. Also, contact banks, stock brokers, and investment houses that offer IRA and Keogh Plan programs.

Quick Tips

✓ Keep complete, accurate records of all transactions to be summarized on your tax returns. Get in the habit of keeping these records in a timely manner so that you do not get behind and confused.

✓ Business taxes are not a good place to practice do-it-yourself techniques. Unless you are well-versed in tax matters, seek the advice of a qualified tax person (fees are tax deductible).

28 Employee payroll taxes

I have been discouraging you from hiring people if you have little money to start. One reason is to control ongoing expenses when you cannot afford them. Another reason is to eliminate the amount of tax paperwork and withholdings you would have to collect.

If you must hire people for your business, there will be no way around payroll taxes. Bite the bullet, dig in, and get the paperwork done. You will find that setting up the tax system is the most difficult part. After that, you should establish a routine to keep employees' records up to date, collect withholdings, and file reports with both federal and state tax authorities.

Before we discuss employee taxes, let's look at other ways you can get help:

- You can use family members. However, there could be some tax implications, depending on the length of time you use family members and how they are used. I suggest you contact your tax adviser if you have any questions.

- You can hire independent contractors to perform specific work. You can work through an employment agency specializing in temporary help, or you can seek someone like yourself who is self-employed. There will be paperwork. You must keep track of payments and file Form 1099-MISC for each independent contractor to whom you paid $600 or more a year, or any independent sales agent who buys $5,000 or more of your products. Forward these forms to the IRS along with Form 1096, "Annual Summary and Transmittal of U.S. Information Returns."

I should also mention that the IRS makes the final decision about whether someone is your employee or an independent contractor. You cannot hire people and call them independent contractors to get around the paperwork. If you were challenged by the IRS, and they decide you have an employer-employee relationship, you will have to submit proper paperwork AND forward the money you should have been withholding.

- You can exchange services with other small business people. For example, you provide your services to a freelance artist who designs an advertisement for you. The IRS expects each participant to file Federal Forms 1099-MISC and 1096 to report these agreements. Use "fair market values" for the services rendered. That is, if you would have charged a client $200 for your service, that is the amount you should show on the forms.

The basic payroll taxes

If you hire people, you will be involved with the following basic taxes:

Federal income tax (also known as F.W.T. - Federal Wage Tax). Usually you will withhold a certain amount from each salary for federal income tax payment. You will forward this money to the IRS on a set schedule.

State income taxes. Most states also have an income tax. Most follow the federal form, but rates will vary. Contact your state's tax revenue department.

Social Security tax (also known as **FICA** - Federal Insurance Contributions Act). You will withhold 7.65% of each employee's wages (up to $53,400 in 1991). In addition, you, the employer, must match that amount.

Federal unemployment tax (FUTA). This money is collected to provide a pool for unemployment payments to workers who have lost their jobs. Your employees do not pay for this—you do. The rules by which small businesses must pay this tax are not simple. I suggest you contact your tax advisor or local IRS office for guidance. You can also review IRS Publication 334 and Circular E. The present tax rate is 6.2% on the first $7,000 of each employee's wages. However, you are given a credit of up to 5.4% for any state unemployment taxes you must pay. In most states, this usually means the federal government gets .8%.

State unemployment taxes. Taxes vary among states. Contact your state's unemployment insurance department.

Setting up payroll federal tax records

This is not meant to be a complete list of your tax obligations. Rather, it is intended to give you an idea of your tax obligations when you become an employer.

- Secure a copy of federal Form S, "Application for Employer Identification Number," from your nearest IRS office. Fill it out and return it to the IRS office. Your business will be assigned a Federal Employer Identification Number.

- From the IRS, secure copies of federal Form W-4, "Employee's Withholding Allowance Certificate." Employees must fill out a form to show their number of exemptions. Keep these forms in your files.

- By January 31 of each year, you must provide a W-2 form to each employee showing the previous year's total wages, withholdings for federal and state income taxes, and withholdings for Social Security.

- By the end of February, you must forward copies of the W-2 forms and a summary form W-3 to the IRS.

- You must forward deducted Social Security taxes at least four times a year to the IRS. You do this by depositing the money in an IRS-authorized bank. Due dates are the end of January, April, July, and October. You will have to pay more frequently if you have a large payroll. Use federal Form 941, "Federal Payroll Tax Returns."

- By January 31, you will probably have to report Federal Unemployment Taxes using Form 940, "Employer's Annual Federal Unemployment Tax Return." If you have accumulated more than $100 in a quarter, you must deposit the money in an authorized bank by the end of January, April, July, and October. If it is less than $100, you can add it to the taxes to be paid the next quarter.

State payroll tax records

State requirements vary, but procedures and schedules generally follow the federal requirements. Check with the appropriate state agencies.

Quick Tips

✓ By now you can see that hiring people can cause a tremendous paperwork burden on the new small business. Let me repeat what I have said several times. If you are on a very limited budget, avoid hiring people until you have experience and enough funds.

✓ As mentioned in Lesson 21, if you incorporate your business, you will be treated as an employee of the corporation and the paperwork in this section will apply to you, too.

✓ Although it is not a tax, I must mention Workers' Compensation Insurance. In most states, you will be required to provide protection for your employees against work-related injuries or death. You, the employer, must pay for this. Premiums will vary by state and job risk.

✓ When you start hiring, get help from the IRS and state agencies and your accountant.

✓ The IRS has several good, free references. If your business is a sole proprietorship, I recommend getting "Your Business Tax Kit," number YBTK-S from the IRS. See the end of Lesson 26 for more tax reference material available from the IRS.

If you think you can do it, you are right.
If you think you cannot do it, you are still right. - Henry Ford

Section G

Starting your Mini-biz™

Nothing will take the place of persistence. Talent will not; nothing is more common than unsuccessful people with talent. Genius will not; unrewarded genius is almost a proverb. Education will not; the world is full of educated derelicts. Persistence and determination are omnipotent. - Calvin Coolidge

29 Naming your Mini-biz

Does your Mini-biz need a name?

Your business probably does not need a unique name if you are selling products of a well-known company, such as Avon or Shaklee. It also may not if you are working at home for another company or if you are working summers or part-time doing jobs such as mowing lawns.

Actually, in these cases your business does have a name—yours. If people are contacting you about your business, or making checks out to you, your name is also the business name.

On the other hand, your business should have a separate name if you are dealing directly with customers to sell your own products or services. It also makes it easier to keep your personal finances separate from those of the business.

Naming your business

Take time to think of a good name. Select one that people will remember and will help sell your products or services. You may decide to use your own name, and call it the "The John B. Smith Company." However, you may want to use a name that gives the impression that the business is somehow different from you. You may want a name that describes and helps promote your business. "Evergreen Lawn Care" is much more descriptive than the "John B. Smith Company."

Quick Tips

✓ Avoid using names that might be confused with the big corporations. Even if your name is George Erickson, avoid the temptation to use "GE Service Company."

✓ Do not claim to be something you are not. Do not say you are the "ABC Manufacturing Company" if you are not a manufacturer, or the "XYZ Institute" if you are not an institute.

✓ Check to see if someone else is already using the same name.

- If you will be operating in a local area, check with your city or county clerk. They should have a list of all local businesses by name.

- If you plan to do business nationally (for example, mail order) you will want to know if another company is using the name. Check with your local library. If they have a business section, they should have a Dun and Bradstreet listing of most U.S. companies.

✓ Register your company with your state or local government.

Requirements vary from state to state. In general, you will always have to register if you are "Doing Business As" (DBA) a name other than your own. Some states or cities require you to register your business even if you use your own name. There is usually a small charge ($5 to $25) to register.

It is better to wear out than to rust out - Bishop George Horne

30 Startup purchases

It is very important that you control initial expenses. The best way to accomplish this is to follow these rules:

- Buy only what you really need—make do with what you have. If you rarely need a particular item, consider renting it.

- Pay the lowest price to get the quality you need. It is important that you understand what I am saying here. I am not saying to buy the cheapest—period. I am saying to look at the quality of what you are buying to make sure it fits your business needs. Let me give you a simple example. I believe that everyone in business should have business cards. If you were selling firewood door-to-door, you could probably use the cheapest card you could find. If you were selling a professional service, you would want a card that projects a strong, professional image. Chances are you would have to pay more for the second type of card. As another example, for some businesses, you could work from your kitchen table. In other businesses, where clients came to your home, you might require a business-like desk.

I divide purchases you might have to make into four categories: equipment, furniture and fixtures, business supplies, and inventory.

Equipment

My definition of equipment includes both production and office equipment. That is, any machinery you need to get your work done. It could be a sewing machine, a personal computer, a power saw, or a truck, to name just a few. As I have said before, equipment tends to be expensive. Therefore, you probably have to own it before starting your Mini-biz.

Keep in mind that equipment may need repairs which can put a strain on your finances. However, repairs are tax deductible. Speaking of taxes, you may be able to depreciate the cost of the equipment, even if it is not new. Discuss this with your tax advisor or call your local IRS office.

Office equipment deserves special attention. Almost all businesses will need access to a telephone. Without one, you could lose a great deal of business. To start, you can use your home phone. However, the telephone company will expect you to install a business phone if you use it for frequent calls. They charge more for that phone service.

An answering machine will give you the ability to receive messages at any time. An inexpensive one is a worthwhile purchase. You may want to purchase one that gives you the date and time of each call.

Depending on your business, you may need a typewriter. If you need one, shop around. With the growth of personal computers, many business typewriters have become surplus. You should be able to find a good used one at a reasonable price.

Furniture and fixtures

Furniture and fixtures include office and production desks, benches, chairs, and cabinets. Before you buy, look around your home for things you can use to get started. Check charity warehouse stores, surplus outlets, and newspaper classifieds for bargains. The fancy trimmings can come later, when you are well established.

Business supplies

Business supplies include stationery items such as pens, paper, staples, and postage stamps. This is another area for economy. Buy only what you need, and shop for the best prices. Because of their importance to almost every business, I am listing the following items separately so you do not forget to consider them. You decide which items you need for your business.

- Business cards
- Some form of sales slip or book of sales slips
- Ledger sheets or books
- Business letters and envelopes

If you are really in a bind for money and you believe you do not need to enhance your business image, you can consider using a rubber stamp with your company name, address, and phone number to start.

Inventory

For our purposes, inventory can be described in three ways:

- Products you buy and have on hand for resale
- Products you make and have on hand for resale
- Raw materials you have on hand to make products for resale

Inventory is a factor in businesses where you buy merchandise for resale. In other words, you have to spend money now, but will not have money coming in until some time later. You will need to control how much and how fast you spend. Part of that control will be based on how fast you can sell. When you buy a finished product, you can sell it immediately. If you must make it first, production time and quantity have to be included.

It is because of potential money problems that some people prefer to operate businesses where they are selling products that do not have to be stocked as inventory. They do this by selling products that are delivered after the sale is made. I cover this in detail in Catalog C8.

Locating suppliers

Depending on your business, there are two types of suppliers you might be interested in contacting: suppliers of products you can sell, or suppliers of raw materials or components of products that you plan to make and then sell.

Sources for products. If you want to buy products at wholesale so that you can sell them, here are a number of sources you can try.

- **Buy from one of the companies listed in Catalog C7 and C8.** This is probably your easiest way to start. These companies are actively looking for individuals who are interested in selling. Most offer easy and inexpensive starter programs for the beginner. Some offer specialized products, while others are wholesalers offering catalogs of name-brand merchandise.

- **Buy from companies that advertise in opportunity magazines** such as those mentioned in Lesson 11. Please remember that the integrity and dependability of these companies vary. Check them thoroughly before getting involved.

- **Buy directly from other manufacturers**. Choices are endless. The biggest problem you might have is getting manufacturers to sell directly to you. Some do not like to sell the relatively small quantities you will want to buy. Others do not like to sell to a small, unknown customer. But you can always ask! Your best sources for information about manufacturers are the following:

    - **For U.S. manufacturers**: *The Thomas Register of American Manufacturers* and *MacRae's Blue Book*. Both are multi-volume sets listing all major manufacturers by product type. You can usually find them at your local library or Chamber of Commerce.

    - **For overseas manufacturers**: You can work through an importer. One of the best sources for information on importers is *The American Directory of Exporters and Importers*, 38 Park Row, New York, NY 10038. You can also subscribe to the following trade magazines which specialize in foreign products:

      Made in Europe, P.O. Box 174027, D-6, Frankfurt-am-Main, Germany.

      The Importer, East Asia Publishing Company, 2-11 Jingumae, 1-Chome, Shibuya-ku, Tokyo 150 Japan.

      Hong Kong Enterprises, 3rd Floor, Connaught Center, Connaught Road Central, Hong Kong.

- **Buy from wholesalers**. You can find local wholesalers listed in the telephone yellow pages.

- **Check trade and industry publications**. If you have experience in a business, you probably are aware of at least one magazine or newspaper for that type of business. You will find feature articles on new products as well as product advertisements. There are thousands of trade publications covering almost any industry you can name. If you are interested in an industry that is new to you, visit your local library. It will have reference books listing all magazines published in the United States, such as the *Gale Directory of Publications and Broadcast Media*.

- **Visit trade shows.** If you happen to live near a city that is hosting a trade show of interest to you, try to attend to find products you may want to sell. This may be difficult because some shows take rigorous steps to restrict attendance to people in the trade. For some, a business card will get you in.

- **Read business opportunity advertisements in newspapers and business magazines.** Most local newspapers and business magazines have classified advertising sections. Depending on the publication, you may find products for sale in these sections. The Sunday edition of the *New York Times* has good "Business opportunities" and "Merchandise for sale" sections in its classified advertising section. Your local library may have copies.

Sources for raw materials or components. Many of the basic sources for products might also be the sources for components, and I will only cover the differences here:

- Components can be bought from many of the companies I mention in Catalog C2, C3, and C4.

- You can also buy from manufacturers. See *The Thomas Register* and *MacRae's* mentioned earlier.

- In many industries, manufacturers use local distributors to reach small customers. These distributors usually cater to one industry or trade, but will sell material from several manufacturers. Some sell only to businesses, while others will sell to the public. Examples include commercial lumber yards and electrical, plumbing, and auto supply distributors. You can find them listed in your local yellow pages. If you live in a small town, you may want to get a copy of the yellow pages of your nearest large city for more choices.

Working with suppliers

When you select suppliers for products or raw materials, you should not make your selections based on price alone. Remember that your success depends on delivering the products you said you would deliver, and on the schedule you promised. If you have unreliable suppliers, you may be forced to miss some of your commitments. This could be disastrous for a new business. Here is a summary of the key points to look for in a supplier. Do not hesitate to get answers to these questions <u>before</u> you place an order. You may want to get the names of some of the supplier's customers and speak to them.

- **Price.** Are the supplier's prices competitive? Can you afford to pay those prices?
- **Quality.** Does the supplier's quality meet your needs?
- **Reliability.** Are deliveries made as promised?
- **Service.** Is the supplier responsive to your special needs?
- **Terms.** What are the supplier's terms for payments? Will the supplier allow you a grace period before you have to pay? Is there a charge for delivery?

Quick Tips

✓ Control expenses. Buy only what you need. Do not buy more than you need just because you can get a "special deal" on a bigger quantity.

✓ Shop around. Look for the best price. Check discount outlets and used equipment suppliers.

✓ Bargains are wonderful—but make sure you get the quality you need. Otherwise, it is no bargain!

There is no security on this earth. Only opportunity -
General Douglas MacArthur

31 Pricing: what to charge

How much are you going to charge for your products or services? This is not an easy question to answer, but it is very important that you spend time on your pricing strategy. If you charge too much, you will not get enough customers. If you charge too little, you will not make enough profit from each sale. In both cases, the business would not give you enough money to pay you for your time and effort.

Big companies have whole departments working to maximize profits. They use powerful computers to track sales, costs, and many other critical business activities. As a small business owner, your first efforts should be to make a reasonable profit. Later, as your business grows, you can work on maximizing them.

The easiest way to price

First of all, you may not have to worry about pricing. If you are using a program provided by another company, they may provide you with "suggested prices." You still may have the option of charging more or less, depending on the demand for your products or services, as well as what your competition charges.

A second easy method is to base your prices on what your competitors charge. This can be a good way to start and learn. If your products are better than your competitors', you may want to charge more. If your products are the same quality, you may want to charge the same—or consider charging less to get started. If you use this method, you still need to review your costs to make sure you are making a profit.

Pricing based on costs

Pricing based on costs is much more complicated, and books have been written on the subject. What I am providing is a simplified description to help you understand. To arrive at a price based on costs, you calculate all costs and then add the profit you want to make. There are several factors you have to consider: direct costs, overhead costs, and profit.

Direct Costs

Direct costs are the costs to make or buy each specific product, or to perform a service. These costs go up as you make more units. If you are selling:

- Products you make. Direct costs are the costs of materials and labor to assemble each product. You should figure a cost of your labor even if you are the only person making the items.

- Products you buy. Direct costs are the costs of each product you buy, including any shipping costs you pay.

- A service. Direct costs are the labor costs to perform a job, plus the costs of any materials used for the job (paint, lumber, fabric, etc.).

Overhead Costs

Overhead costs are general business expenses required to run the business. They tend to be "fixed costs" in that you must pay the same amount regardless of the number of units you make or sell. To recover these costs, you will have to average them across the number of units you sell. There are many possible overhead costs. Here are a few:

- Salaries not part of direct costs
- Business taxes, including payroll taxes
- Office and shop supplies
- Rent (this might be a part of your home—see Lesson 27)
- Telephone and utilities (see Lesson 27)
- Cost or depreciation of equipment
- Car or truck expenses
- Advertising
- Accountant or lawyer fees

Selling costs

Selling costs are the costs associated with the actual selling of your products. Depending on how you run your business, selling costs could be either direct or overhead costs. If you pay salespeople by commission for each item they sell, the commissions would be direct costs. If you hire salespeople and pay them a fixed salary, these would usually be overhead costs.

Profit

Profit is what drives most businesses, large or small. It is your reward for all your hard work. I can give two simplified definitions. First, profit is the money left after you subtract all costs from your selling price. Looking at it differently, profit is the amount of money you should add to your costs to assure your business is making money.

The following statement may seem obvious, but it is an important point to make: for your business to be profitable, your individual products or services must be profitable. Some products will probably be more profitable than others (and some might even lose money until you can sell them off), but the total of your effort should be a profit for the business. Therefore, profit should be calculated at the product or service level.

Here is another key point. The profit you expect to make will be influenced by the "turnover rate" of your inventory—that is, how fast you sell products. For example, supermarkets operate with low profit margins per item to remain competitive. However, with a high number of daily transactions, the turnover rates for many products are high. They might sell hundreds of a single product in one day. Compare this operation to a small hobby shop that must carry many items that have a very low turnover rate. Some items may sit on the shelves for months. With relatively few transactions per day, this shopkeeper must make more profit per item to survive.

A method for pricing based on costs

Let's work through a simple approach to show how you would derive a selling price. In this case, you are manufacturing widgets:

1. Estimate how many widgets you expect to sell in one month.

2. Estimate your monthly overhead costs.

3. Divide:

   $$\frac{\text{Monthly Overhead Cost (item 2)}}{\text{Monthly Widget Unit Sales (item 1)}} = \text{Overhead per Widget}$$

4. Estimate direct cost per unit

5. Add:

   Direct Cost (item 4) + Overhead per Widget (item 3) = Cost per Widget

6. Estimate Percentage of Profit you want (let's say 25%—a reasonable percent for many businesses)

7. Multiply:

   .25 (item 6) X Cost per Widget (item 5) = Profit

8. Add:

   Cost per Widget (item 5) + Profit (item 7) = Selling Price

When you have calculated the selling price, you may want to adjust it up or down to achieve a price that is easy to work with or that people are used to. For example, if your calculated price came out as $2.87, you may want to use $2.98, a more common pricing technique.

Other factors you should consider

The demand for your products or services. If people really want to buy what you are selling, perhaps you can charge more.

What competitors charge. You cannot price your product without considering competition. If competition is strong, you may have to charge less to build a customer base. This presents two questions:

- Can you live with the lower prices? (That is, can you make enough profit?)

- If not, what advantages do you offer that will allow you to raise prices after you have been in business a while?

The condition of the national or local economy. If potential customers are watching their expenses, you may have to price lower to get their interest and to get them to buy. In good times, people are more willing to pay higher prices.

Customers' perception. What people think of your products or services can affect how you price. Your price for a product must be consistent with what people are willing to pay for it. They simply will not buy if they think your product is not worth your asking price.

Businesses use pricing as part of their marketing strategies. The high prices associated with some perfumes, cars, and sports equipment convey the idea that higher prices mean better. "Prestige pricing" sends a message of status and quality. At the other end of pricing strategies, pricing low sends a message of thrift and good value. Obviously, a business that prices low must sell more units to make the same total profit as a business that prices high.

For a business, the best of both worlds would be to price high, establish a reputation that creates demand, and then sell big volumes. We have seen this happen with some high-priced car and clothing manufacturers.

Quick Tips

✓ Remember, the main purpose of pricing is to achieve a reasonable profit for a business. Pricing can be influenced by many factors. Some factors you cannot control, but you should be aware of them and take them into consideration in your pricing strategy.

✓ Use a simple pricing approach to get started. As you grow and learn, you can experiment to improve your profit picture.

Success is simply a matter of luck. Ask any failure - Earl Wilson

First decide what you want to do, then have all the courage to start towards the goal, no matter how impossible it looks. If you want to get there badly enough, nothing can stop you - Henry Kaiser

32 Selecting your selling approach

Do you know how you are going to sell your products or services? Almost any Mini-biz you choose will require you to spend some of your time selling. In some businesses, selling will take most of your time, in others, only a small amount of time. In all cases, selling is a critical activity if you want to make your business a success. There are dozens of ways you can sell. Some will work for your business and some will not. Before you start the business, you must know how you intend to sell, or the ways you intend to try.

Exercise 7 on the following pages lists many ways to sell. The list can never be complete, so feel free to add new approaches that may be appropriate for your business. Then decide what would be the best way to sell to <u>your</u> customers. Even if you know how you intend to sell, spend time looking over the list for new ideas. Additional selling approaches could mean more business for you. You should review this exercise from time to time.

Exercise instructions

1. Write down what you will be selling—your products or services—and a short description of your typical customer (see Lesson 16). Refer to these descriptions as you consider ways you can sell.

2. In the left column, check the boxes for any sales approach you plan to use when you start your business. In the right column, check the boxes for any approach you would like to try at some time after you start. Use a pencil so that you can make changes.

3. If you check a box, you can write any specific ideas you have on the line next to it.

Exercise 7 — Selecting your selling approach

Your products or services are ______________________________

____

Your typical customer has these traits ______________________________

____

How and where are you going to sell?

Plan to use / Would like to try — DESCRIPTION

- ☐ ☐ In your home or garage ______________________________
- ☐ ☐ Door-to-door ______________________________
- ☐ ☐ Home parties ______________________________
- ☐ ☐ Telephone ______________________________
- ☐ ☐ Mail order ______________________________
- ☐ ☐ Fax ______________________________
- ☐ ☐ Bulletin Boards ______________________________
- ☐ ☐ P.T.A.s ______________________________
- ☐ ☐ Youth sports leagues ______________________________
- ☐ ☐ Art and craft shows ______________________________
- ☐ ☐ Fairs ______________________________
- ☐ ☐ Trade shows ______________________________
- ☐ ☐ Sidewalk sales ______________________________
- ☐ ☐ Amusement parks ______________________________
- ☐ ☐ Tourist parks ______________________________

Continued on next page

Exercise 7

Plan to use
Would like to try

DESCRIPTION

- ☐ ☐ Sports events ____________
- ☐ ☐ Flea markets ____________
- ☐ ☐ Beaches ____________
- ☐ ☐ Mall booths ____________
- ☐ ☐ Home and garden shows ____________
- ☐ ☐ Rent space in a store ____________
- ☐ ☐ Tourist attractions ____________
- ☐ ☐ College dorms ____________
- ☐ ☐ Other ____________
- ☐ ☐ Other ____________
- ☐ ☐ Other ____________

If you are selling to "middlemen," you may also want to consider:

Plan to use
Would like to try

DESCRIPTION

- ☐ ☐ Independent selling agents ____________
- ☐ ☐ On consignment ____________
- ☐ ☐ Rack merchandising ____________
- ☐ ☐ Vending machines ____________
- ☐ ☐ Other ____________
- ☐ ☐ Other ____________
- ☐ ☐ Other ____________

He started to sing as he started the thing
That couldn't be done and he did it - Edgar Guest

33 How are you going to advertise?

You can have the best product or service in the world, but if potential customers are not aware of your Mini-biz and what you have to offer, you probably will not succeed. Working with a small budget can limit what you can do to promote your business. However, there are still many things you can try. It is important that you do something, and I will give you a number of inexpensive techniques to consider.

There are many ways a business can reach potential customers. For our purposes, promoting your business can take two forms:

- Advertising
- Publicity

The two should work together, and sometimes it is difficult to tell them apart. This lesson discusses advertising. The next lesson discusses ways you can promote your Mini-biz through publicity.

Let's say you intend to sell directly at craft shows. You can quickly find out how much it will cost to rent space. You will also want to know if a booth or table is supplied. If not, you will have to provide your own. Next, you want to have attractive decorations and signs to draw buyers to your booth. This may cost money, depending on how much you can do yourself. Many exhibitors go no further. If you are smart, you will also have business cards and a simple sheet or brochure promoting your products. This gives potential customers your name and phone number if they want to contact you later to buy. There is much more you can do to get the word out about you and your Mini-biz.

Advertising

Advertising can be described as paid promotion through which you tell potential customers about your business and what you are selling. The most common forms are television, radio, magazine, and newspaper advertisements. They can be very expensive and beyond the budget of a new Mini-biz. However, here are some approaches that may fit your needs and budget.

Inexpensive ways to advertise

Word of mouth. The very least you should do is to tell people about your business. Start with family members and friends, but do not stop there. Ask them to tell others for you. Once you have satisfied customers, ask them for the names of other people who might be interested in what you are selling.

Business cards. You may not consider business cards as advertising, but few businesses can do without them. As you start, they can be used in several ways to advertise if you can describe what you are selling in a few words. Some people use a folded card to provide more information. You can give cards to friends and anyone you meet. Some restaurants, bars, and stores provide a rack or bulletin board where you can leave cards. Keep cards with you at all times and do not hesitate to give them to people. They will give you a chance to talk about your Mini-biz, and that could mean more sales.

Flyers. This is one of the least expensive ways to advertise locally. You design—or have someone design—a simple, single sheet describing what you are selling. Make sure your phone number is easy to find. Have copies printed at a local print or copy center, and put them on car windshields, home mail boxes, or apartment doors. For a large circulation you can use your own or neighborhood teenagers to deliver them.

Flyers plus. If you are selling a product from a known manufacturer, here is a clever way to enhance your flyer. Many manufacturers have attractive fact sheets describing their products. Sometimes, they are in full color. Try to buy a supply of these from the manufacturer at low cost. Then staple your flyer to the fact sheet and distribute them. I have seen this technique used for such products as water filters and home outdoor lighting systems.

Newspaper inserts. If you live in a small city, you may be able to negotiate to insert your flyer into a daily newspaper. Some newspapers will even "zone" the inserts, so that they will only be delivered to certain areas of the city.

Classified advertisements in local newspapers. Depending on what you are selling, these ads can be very effective. The key is to make sure the paper has an ad category that matches what you are selling. People read these ads because they are looking for a solution to a problem. They will only look in those sections that they believe will provide help.

"Weekly Shoppers" advertising. This is another low-cost approach. What I said about newspaper classified ads applies here as well.

College and school newspapers. If you have a product of interest to students, these newspaper rates are very reasonable.

Cooperative advertising. Many businesses cannot afford to advertise on their own. Co-op advertising allows a number of businesses to work together to produce a common mailing. Quite often, the mailings offer discount coupons.

House signs. Place a small, attractive sign in front of your home. Caution: Before you do, check local zoning restrictions.

Truck and auto signs. Putting a sign on a vehicle broadcasts your business wherever you go. If you do not want a permanent sign, you can buy a magnetic one that can be attached or removed in seconds.

Signs on trees and lamp posts. If you do seasonal work, you may be able to attach signs or flyers to street trees and lamp posts. City officials may frown on this practice, but the signs still appear.

"Work in progress" signs. If you work at someone's home or yard, ask if you can display a sign while you are working there. This is a common practice with house painters and other home improvement specialists. Be sure to include your telephone number.

Telephone marketing (or telemarketing). This can be a very time-consuming activity. However, a personal phone call can be very effective for some businesses. For others, it is essential. For example, if your business requires having just a few big customers, you would be wise to spend an hour a day on the phone prospecting for customers.

Another telephone approach that is gaining in popularity is to use a special tape recorder with an auto-dial capability. You enter a batch of phone numbers to call, and the system does the rest by playing your pre-recorded message. Do not use this technique to reach important clients. It is too impersonal.

Direct mail campaigns. You mail letters directly to possible customers. Because of preparation and mailing costs, it works best when you only need a few big customers.

Mail order. This is a special case, discussed in Catalog C9.

Advertising specialties. You can purchase inexpensive "giveaway" items with your business name and telephone number on them. Inexpensive items include pencils and key rings. Check in your telephone yellow pages.

Telephone "yellow pages." If you can afford it, advertising in the telephone classified directory can be one of your best ways to reach customers for many businesses. The cost will vary by city. Since they are only published once a year, you have to work to their schedule. If your business products or services appeal to college students, many colleges have directories that are less expensive than city ones.

Radio and television advertising. In most cases, these are well beyond the budgets of anyone looking to start with very little money. This is especially true of TV, with its big production expenses. If you are a smooth promoter and have a good product, you might consider trying a "per inquiry" approach with a local station (see Catalog C9).

After you have studied the various ways you can advertise, do Exercise 8, on page 143, to help you decide how you will advertise your Mini-biz.

In good times, people want to advertise; in bad times, they have to - Bruce Barton

34 Promoting a Mini-biz with publicity

For our purposes, I describe publicity as "free advertising" for your business. Its goals are to create an awareness and interest in you and your business and to leave a positive impression. The word "free" can be misleading. Although a newspaper article or television interview may be free, you will probably have to spend time and some money to get the article or interview.

Publicity may not seem as important as advertising for a Mini-biz. However, a good publicity campaign can do wonders for <u>any</u> business. Notice how many TV talk shows have celebrities as guests who are there to promote their book, or movie, or upcoming TV show. You should do the same for your Mini-biz. After you have reviewed the following techniques, do Exercise 8 to focus on your Mini-biz.

Inexpensive publicity techniques

Word of mouth. Certainly some of the best publicity you can have is satisfied customers who tell others about you. The quality of your products and services can be an important promotional tool.

Newspaper articles. Newspapers are eager to find stories about local people and businesses. But it must be "newsworthy"—there must be something new and different to make it an interesting story. If you want a newspaper story, you must take the initiative to make it happen. If you have something really exciting, contact your local newspaper, and they may have you meet with a reporter or feature writer. However, it is much more likely that you will have to do most of the work by creating a press release. This is a story that you write and submit so that the editor can use it with only minor changes. Write about yourself and your company as if you were a reporter. Do not use "I" or "my," but write about "Mr. or Ms. Jones." There are specific guidelines on writing a press release. If interested, contact your local library for a good book on the subject.

Write newspaper or magazine articles. If you have expertise, you can submit articles to your local newspaper or a magazine. Concentrate on small, specialized magazines. The big ones have their own staffs, or only use name authors. You probably will not be paid very well, but your main interest is getting exposure that could help your business.

Radio and television interviews. An interview on a local television or radio station can be great publicity. You will need to have an interesting and timely topic and be able to speak well and answer impromptu questions. Decide what interview show you are interested in, and contact its producer or host. The best way is to first send a short, business-like letter. State your topic, your expertise and credentials, and why you think you would be of interest to listeners. Follow this with a telephone call.

Public speaking. If you can speak well, there are always opportunities to talk to professional, civic, or social clubs. You must have an interesting topic that will appeal to your audience, and your speech should not be just an advertisement for your business. Remember, you are speaking as an expert who happens to own a business. Do not forget to have your business cards with you. Contact the club's president or program director and volunteer your services.

Join clubs and organizations. Depending on the type of your business, joining related clubs can be important for two reasons. You can learn from other members, and you can "network" by meeting people you can help and who can help you. Membership fees may be tax deductible.

Charitable donations. Donating your products or services to a worthy cause will let people know about your business in a very positive way. At the same time, you will feel good helping others. Donations are tax deductible.

Your business image. This is an extra item that will influence how people think about you and your business. When it comes to such items as business cards and stationary, buy the best you can afford so you create the image you want to project. How you dress and act are also important (see Lesson 35).

Exercise 8

Your advertising and publicity

This exercise will allow you to take what you have learned in the last two lessons and apply the information to your Mini-biz.

In the left column, check the boxes of the advertising and publicity approaches you intend to try when you start your Mini-biz. In the right column, check those you hope to try in the future. Use a pencil so that you can make changes.

Advertising

You must have a plan for advertising, even if it is by word of mouth. People must know about your Mini-biz before they can buy. Spend time on the following list to decide what is best for you.

Plan to use
Would like to try

Specific actions planned

☐ ☐ Word of mouth - *Provide quality products and services, and this will happen!*

☐ ☐ Business cards ____________________

☐ ☐ Flyers ____________________

☐ ☐ Flyers plus ____________________

☐ ☐ Newspaper inserts ____________________

☐ ☐ Classified advertisements ____________________

☐ ☐ "Weekly shopper" advertising ____________________

☐ ☐ College and school newspapers ____________________

☐ ☐ Cooperative advertising ____________________

☐ ☐ House signs ____________________

☐ ☐ Truck and auto signs ____________________

☐ ☐ Signs on trees and lamp posts ____________________

☐ ☐ "Work in progress" signs ____________________

☐ ☐ Telephone marketing ____________________

☐ ☐ Direct mail campaigns ____________________

Exercise 8

Plan to use
Would like to try

Specific actions planned

☐ ☐ Mail order ____________________

☐ ☐ Advertising specialties ____________________

☐ ☐ Telephone "yellow pages" ____________________

☐ ☐ Radio advertising ____________________

☐ ☐ Television advertising ____________________

☐ ☐ Other ____________________

☐ ☐ Other ____________________

Publicity

You should always look for opportunities to tell people about your business. Pursuing one or more of the following approaches could bring you a great deal of business. Be creative and persistent!

Plan to use
Would like to try

Specific actions planned

☐ ☐ Newspaper articles ____________________

☐ ☐ Radio interviews ____________________

☐ ☐ Television interviews ____________________

☐ ☐ Public speaking ____________________

☐ ☐ Join clubs and organizations ____________________

☐ ☐ Charitable donations ____________________

☐ ☐ Other ____________________

☐ ☐ Other ____________________

Hoping and waiting is not my way of doing things - Johann von Goethe

35 Overcoming startup problems

The problem

When you first start, you may have to work extra hard to demonstrate that you are capable and that your business is legitimate. After all, you have no record of accomplishments and no satisfied customers to use for references. For some businesses this is no problem. For others, it can be a serious obstacle.

Some solutions

First, your appearance

- For <u>any</u> business, you must look the part. When you meet customers, dress to fit the situation. Depending on your business, this could mean a business suit or jeans or something else.

- Be neat in your personal appearance and with what you are selling or demonstrating. Neatness always pays.

- <u>Always</u> be pleasant and business-like. Remember, a satisfied customer can give you repeat business and refer you to friends.

Your approach

- Study to make sure you know your business. Project confidence when you talk to customers.

- Listen to the customer and understand what he or she really needs. Then sell to that need.

- Promise the minimum that will make the customer happy—but deliver more than you promise. This is bound to please customers! Again, remember you need both new and repeat business. Pleased customers will tell their friends about you AND will also buy from you again.

Note: This advice is good for <u>any</u> business, established or new.

Sales promotions

Since you are new to the market, you may have to do something to get the attention of potential customers and encourage them to buy from you. We discussed ways to advertise and get publicity in lessons 33 and 34. However, using these techniques will only let people know you are in business. How are you going to motivate them to try your products or services? The best way to do this is through sales promotions, which are special incentives to stimulate business. Here are a few examples:

1. You can reduce prices. Make sure your advertising states you are reducing prices. Take nothing for granted.

2. You can have a buy-one-get-one-free sale.

3. You can offer a money-back guarantee. If you are performing a service, you can ask for a very small deposit with the rest to be paid upon satisfactory completion of work.

4. If you are selling to stores, you can place products on consignment. That is, you do not get paid until the item is sold. This eliminates the risk for the store owner.

Quick Tips

✓ Try this quick test. Look in a mirror and practice selling. Would <u>you</u> listen to, trust, and buy from that person in the mirror?

✓ If used with a good advertising campaign, price promotions should "prime the pump" to get sales started. On the other hand, your profits will suffer. It is important to watch price promotions carefully and return to normal pricing as soon as possible.

Don't find fault. Find a remedy - Henry Ford

36 Record keeping

Whatever your business, you should keep good records. In fact, the IRS expects you to. The records need not be very fancy, but they must be complete and accurate. If you want to run a successful business—rather than have a business that runs you—you must keep track of what is happening. Good record keeping habits will put you in that position.

If you are familiar with bookkeeping or accounting, you should already know what I am about to tell you. If you are not familiar, we could have a problem. This book is not meant to describe all the concepts and terms involved. If you have any money to spare, I recommend you spend it to hire a good accountant to get you started in the right direction. You can also take bookkeeping courses at a vocational school. For a very good business book for small business owners, see the Quick Tips at the end of this lesson.

If you have no additional money, or feel you would like to try the business before hiring an accountant, I will describe a basic system you can use when starting. If anyone should ask, I will be describing a *single-entry system based on the accrual accounting method*. This is the simplest system that is acceptable to the IRS for most small businesses that carry inventory. It will provide a simple money-in/money-out record for daily transactions, as well as monthly and yearly totals. As the business grows and money comes in, I strongly recommend you hire a good accountant as soon as you can afford it. Here's how the system works.

Selling transactions

Daily sales. Keep a record of each sale during the day. This could take several forms, depending on your business and the number of daily sales. For example:

- If you are selling a service, or selling to a business that will pay later, you probably would use an invoice.
- A low-volume business might use a sales slip. These often can be purchased in booklet form.
- A high-volume business might use a cash register.

In each of these cases, you need two copies, one for the customer, the other for your records. If you use a cash register, get one that can print the second copy.

In some cases, you may not give customers a receipt. This might happen at fairs and flea markets. You should keep a list of daily sales in a "Cash" book, which can be purchased at stationery stores. If you are selling low-cost, high-volume items, you may be basing your total sales on the daily cash receipts without a record of individual sales.

There are several styles of each of these sales forms available. Visit a stationery supply store and pick the one that suits you. To be business-like, you may want to have them printed with your company name. It is also very desirable to have them sequentially numbered. When you fill out a sales form, record the sales tax separately. Then add the tax to the base price to get the total sale price.

At the end of the day. Total the day's sale and tax receipts. Enter the total in a monthly *income ledger*. Again, these are available in several forms at stationery stores. A page provides space to summarize a month of daily sales.

At the end of the month. Add the totals for sales and taxes for the month in the income ledger.

Business purchases

Daily. Keep copies of invoices for all business purchases. If it is an inexpensive purchase, you may want to pay it from "petty cash." You still need to keep a record of the purchase.

At the end of the day. Record details on each purchase made that day in an *expenditure ledger* (from stationery stores). For tax purposes, you will have to separate different types of expenditures. Purchase ledger forms that will help you to make this separation as you enter them.

At the end of each month. Add up monthly totals and enter them in the expenditure ledger.

Profit and Loss statement

Sometimes called the "Income Statement" or "P & L Statement," this is your business's report card you prepare each month and year. From it, you can quickly tell how well the business is doing. Its concept is very simple:

	Money In	(taken from your income ledger)
minus	Money Out	(taken from your expenditure ledger)
equals	Profit	(If this is a negative number, then there is a loss)

In practice, it can be more complicated, especially if you have expenses such as product or materials inventory. When you prepare a monthly statement, you should also calculate the profit or loss for the year-to-date. With the monthly and year-to-date figures, you will have a good idea of how the business is progressing. If you are concerned about the future, I recommend you prepare a cash-flow analysis as described in Lesson 19, Exercise 5.

Quick Tips

✓ There are several simplified bookkeeping ledgers available. A popular one is the Dome Simplified Monthly Bookkeeping record. It costs about ten dollars at stationary stores.

✓ If you own a personal computer, there are several programs that make bookkeeping easier and less prone to errors.

✓ With growth, you will probably have to convert over to a more comprehensive bookkeeping system.

✓ As your business grows, remember what I said about a getting an accountant. It can pay off in savings in tax dollars, or less hassle with the IRS. And any charges are tax deductible.

✓ For a more detailed explanation of bookkeeping—and many other aspects of running your own business, I recommend the book *Small-Time Operator* by Bernard Kamoroff, published by Bell Springs Publishing, Box 640 Bell Springs Road, Laytonville, CA 95454.

When you can measure what you are speaking about, and express it in numbers, you know something about it; but if you cannot measure it, knowledge is of a meager and unsatisfactory kind - Lord Kelvin

Section H

Making your Mini-biz grow

Anyone, in any walk of life, who is content with mediocrity is untrue to himself and to the American tradition - General George Patton

37 How to make your Mini-biz grow

Once you have your business started, you should immediately start thinking about ways to make it grow. You have planted the seed—now you want the business to grow and blossom. The experience you gain and the money you earn can open up endless opportunities for you.

Someone once said the only constant is change. Even the rate of change is changing, so we are experiencing major changes more frequently. Change brings opportunity. Keep your eyes open and desire burning and there will be no limits to what you can achieve.

What you should do right away

1. Make customer satisfaction a key goal.

- Establish your business reputation for quality and guarantee your products and services.
- Do what you say—promise the least that will make the customer happy, but deliver the most that you can. Deliver when you said you would.
- In short, treat customers the way you would like to be treated.

2. Keep profits in the business.

- Use the money to improve or expand product lines or services.
- Do more advertising.

3. **Look for new ways to reach prospects.**

   - Try different ways to advertise and promote your business.

   - Join civic and business groups. Build your network of people who can help you—and whom you can help!

4. **Hire independent agents to sell your products.** Pay by commission.

5. **Don't get greedy—watch your growth.**

   - Do not over-extend or promise what you may not be able to deliver.

   - Start thinking about what additional product lines or services you could <u>slowly</u> add to the present business.

Ways you can grow your Mini-biz

1. **Build up the business you have started.** This will mean watching the company grow and become more complex.

   - Add products or services (see next page).

   - Hire help. You would hire employees for three possible purposes:

     To do the same type of work you are doing (selling, assembling, repairing, counseling, etc.).

     To do the routine chores, such as office work, while you concentrate on what you like and can do best.

     To add a skill or expertise your business needs.

2. **Stay relatively small, but get involved in other small businesses.**

   - For example, add a winter snow removal or firewood business to your summer lawn care business.

3. **Use your Mini-biz to gain experience and funds** to start or buy the business you always wanted.

Adding more product lines to sell

When you want to add more product lines, you will have to decide whether you want to add:

- **Similar product lines:** to give your customers more choices. The customers can choose which products to buy from more than one line.

- **Complementary product lines:** different products than you are now selling, but which would appeal to the same customer. For example, jewelry and cosmetics. Customers may buy different products from more than one line.

- **Unrelated product lines:** very different products from those you are now selling and that may or may not appeal to the same buyer. For example, jewelry and vitamins. In some situations, this may not make good use of your selling time, and therefore it is usually not done. On the other hand, this technique may provide you with some income from one set of products if others are not selling during a period of time. Certain jewelry might sell very well before Christmas and Valentine's Day, but not sell well the rest of the year. Vitamins may sell well all year.

Other money-making opportunities for your business

If you started your business from an original idea, and it is doing well, there are several proven ways to make it pay off even more. Here are some, in order of complexity. You can:

- **Teach classes.** If you have expertise that others would like to learn, you can make arrangements at a vocational school or adult education center to teach a class.

- **Write a book or manual** to fully describe your business. Over the years, hundreds have been written. Many have been self-published and sold by the authors. Quality varies. Some are well-written and nicely printed. Others seem to be thrown together to make quick money. If you are interested in trying to write a book, remember what I said earlier—work toward high quality and customer satisfaction!

- **Develop a startup course** explaining what you did and how you did it. The course should come with complete documentation. It could include from one to three manuals. Some courses available today include audio tapes or video tapes. Courses are priced from $79 to $1000, depending on their complexity and thoroughness.

- **Offer a franchise**. These differ from a course in that you offer many more services, from site selection to a proven inventory-control system. A franchise usually requires the purchaser to use the franchise company's name and products, and set procedures must be followed. Franchising can become a big operation, so it is important to have a proven program before you consider this approach. A number of sloppy programs have resulted in close supervision by the Federal Trade Commission.

No one knows what it is that he can do until he tries - Lucius Seneca

38 Changes you may want to make

As your Mini-biz grows, you should consider several changes to your operations. The Mini-biz concept works by bypassing or limiting some of the steps you would normally take in a typical small business. If you are now making money, you need to protect yourself and your business.

Steps to consider

You should review the following questions every few months to see if there is something you should change. As your business changes, reviews can point out what should be corrected or improved.

1. **Can you improve your advertising?** Are there approaches you can try that might increase business?

2. **Should you change the legal form of your business?** If you started as a proprietorship or partnership, you may want to incorporate for legal and tax reasons.

3. **Should you hire a lawyer to review your business?** Besides looking at the legal form of your Mini-biz, a lawyer may be able to make suggestions to improve your operations and reduce potential liabilities.

4. **Should you hire an accountant?** An accountant can save you a great deal of money by showing you good operating procedures and how to take all tax deductions to which you are entitled.

5. **Should you review your business and personal insurance needs?** Personal and business needs could change. There should be no charge for this review.

6. **Should you consider borrowing money?** Now that you have had experience with your business, you may want to grow faster than you could with your own money.

7. **Should you hire help?** If there is more business than you can handle operating on your own, you should consider hiring full or part-time help.

What we anticipate seldom occurs; what we least expect generally happens - Benjamin Disraeli

Section I

A catalog of Mini-biz opportunities

When I look back on all those worries, I remember the story of the old man who said on his deathbed that he had a lot of worries in his life, most of which never happened. - Winston Churchill

Catalog: Introduction

The following segments of this catalog (C1 to C17) give hundreds of ideas for a business of your own. It cannot be a complete listing since there are thousands and thousands of opportunities to choose from, and the list is growing and changing continuously.

RECOMMENDATION: Before proceeding to look at the opportunities, read Catalog C1, which follows. It explains how the opportunities are divided to make it convenient for you to make the best use of your time.

I have tried to select interesting and unique ideas to stimulate your interest. My aim is to provide something for everyone—regardless of age, educational background, experience, or financial situation. Therefore, many opportunities may not interest you. That's okay. Remember, you only need one opportunity to get started!

As you look through the listings, you may find the perfect opportunity for you. If not, I hope that you will spend time browsing through all the opportunities while giving extra time to those opportunities that are of special interest to you. This could set your imagination working to create a new idea for a Mini-biz.

Companies

When possible, I name companies that provide information, supplies, or a complete program. Some of the companies are very large, with annual sales in billions of dollars. At the other extreme, some are a one-person business—a real, live Mini-biz! What the companies have in common is they all offer low-cost programs or instructional materials.

Some companies require no money to get started; others require up to $1000. I have refrained from including actual charges because some companies frequently change prices and terms. Some companies will run special promotions for a period of time. While there are exceptions, you can expect prices to fall within the following broad ranges:

Books and manuals	$ 5 to $79
Complete training courses	$79 to $795
Full startup programs	0 to $999

A word of caution

I describe many companies and their products. To the best of my knowledge these companies are reputable and financially sound. But conditions change, and so do companies' business conditions, policies, and management. I urge you to investigate and evaluate the present condition of any company offering an opportunity you intend to pursue.

Use good judgment when you evaluate any claims a company makes about how much money you can make. Some claims are just plain ridiculous, and usually involve get-rich-quick schemes. More often, a company will try to make its programs look as attractive as possible by stating the best results that its best clients have achieved. If you are the right person, with the right opportunity, at the right time, you can make a fortune with a Mini-biz. Even with less perfect conditions, you can make a very comfortable living. Just don't assume you will automatically make the amount of money a company claims. For these reasons, I do not include any company claims in this book.

What you can do

When you write to a company, note the quality of the information package it sends to you. Is it poorly printed? Do the company's claims sound too good to be true? Do you get a feeling of confidence from the information package?

Contact the Better Business Bureau in the city where the company does business. Is the company a member of BBB? Does the company have any complaints filed against it?

If you have any questions, write or telephone the company. Ask for names of satisfied customers and contact them.

If you are uncomfortable with a company or its program, look elsewhere!

C1 Types of businesses

Selecting the type of Mini-biz you want is important because each business has unique procedures, requirements, and opportunities. The simplest way that some experts use to categorize businesses is to divide them into two groups. The first is product oriented—these businesses make, distribute, or sell a product. The second is service oriented—these businesses provide assistance or do something for the customer. However, in order to give a more accurate and realistic picture of what might be ahead for you, we need to divide businesses further.

To start, I use five general business categories: Production, Sales, Service, Creative, and Promotional. I then sub-divide each category into a number of basic types. I describe each basic type and its specific opportunities in the following segments of the book, starting with Catalog C2.

But first, let's look at a brief explanation of each category and basic type so that you can focus on and understand those that appeal to you.

Production businesses

Businesses in the **Production** category make products, or components for a product. For our purposes, production includes any product made in quantity. Let's face it. There are many manufacturing operations you will not be able to start because of heavy initial expenses which can run into millions of dollars. On the other hand, there are production businesses you can start as a Mini-biz if you choose wisely. The trick is to select a business with low startup costs for both equipment and raw material. A few examples where this can happen include cloth or wood products, some jewelry, baked goods, and printed products. The basic production types I will use are as follows:

Make to sell. First you make products, then sell them. See Catalog C2 for details.

Make to order. First you get an order for products, then make them. See Catalog C3.

Publish and sell information. You write something (a book, manual, newsletter), have it printed, and sell it yourself. See Catalog C4. I include writing a book that you sell to a publisher under "Creative businesses," on the next page.

Raise to sell. This is similar to make/sell, but you raise animals or grow plants, then sell them. See Catalog C5.

Contract. Another company provides you with components that you assemble into finished products. You return them to the company and get paid for each finished product. See Catalog C6.

Sales businesses

While all businesses require some degree of selling, the **Sales** category is reserved for those businesses in which selling is the primary function. There are two basic types:

Buy to sell. First you buy finished products from a company, then sell them. See Catalog C7.

Sell to order. First you take orders for finished products, then buy and deliver them. See Catalog C8.

How you go about selling is a different consideration. There are dozens of ways to sell, and Lesson 32 provides an extensive list. The following ways to sell have enough unique features to be considered businesses:

Vending machines. You buy and install vending machines and make money selling merchandise from the machines. There are only limited opportunities for a Mini-biz because of initial expenses. Therefore, I have included vending machines with "Sell to order" opportunities in Catalog C8.

Mail order. You sell products or services from your home using the mail. See Catalog C9.

Multi-level Marketing (MLM), also known as **Network Marketing**. You act as an agent of a company to sell its products or services. You also recruit other people to become agents. You receive commissions on the products you sell, as well as on the sales of the agents you recruit, and the agents they recruit, through several levels of agents. See Catalog C10.

Service businesses

Businesses in the **Service** category do something for the benefit of someone else. They can be divided into three categories:

Services for individuals. See Catalog C11.

Services for homes and cars. See Catalog C12.

Services for businesses. See Catalog C13.

Creative businesses

Businesses in the **Creative** category produce original and unique items. For our purposes, we will look at

Creative for resale. You create items that you usually sell one at a time. For example, paintings, ceramics, and a variety of other crafts. See Catalog C14.

Creative for production. You create something that you sell to a company which then mass produces the product and sells it to the public. For example, you could write a book or a song, or invent something, or do art work for greeting cards, or write a computer program, to name a few opportunities. See Catalog C15.

Promotional businesses

In **Promotional** businesses, you act as the coordinator of other people's activities to get things done. For example, you can be the promoter of a craft fair by finding a suitable place, getting exhibitors to show their crafts, and then advertising to get customers to attend. See Catalog C16.

Businesses you can start if you own certain equipment

This is not a separate business category. I have included it for readers who own equipment that could be used in a Mini-biz. See Catalog 17.

Summary

While I have tried to define business types clearly, the distinction among them is not always simple. For example, fast-food shops are generally considered to be service businesses because they perform a service—that is, they quickly provide food to their customers. However, they also sell the food after they prepare it, which is a form of production. But don't worry. Perfect definitions are not required. My prime interest is to get you to think about what has to be done before you commit your time and energy to an opportunity.

How to review the business opportunities

Each of the following segments describes opportunities in one basic business type. I try to present those that are somewhat unusual, since you should be aware of the obvious ones. Take your time in selecting those that best fit your talents, experience, and needs. And remember, the lists may trigger a completely new opportunity you may want to pursue!

When you find an opportunity that appeals to you, write it down in Exercise 10 at the end of this book. The exercise will help you to make the final decision on which business to start.

If you do not think about the future, you cannot have one -
John Galsworthy

C2 Production: Make to sell

Description: You make a number of the same product and then sell them.

Concerns: Do you understand the production process and costs for the product you want to produce? For example, a "cheap" plastic item might require tens of thousands of dollars for tooling. You would need huge manufacturing and sales quantities to repay this cost.

Can you make enough products to meet the demand and give you the income you want?

Do you have a way to sell your output?

Can you manage and afford the inventory of unsold products?

If packaging or displays are required, can you afford quality items that will attract buyers?

Tip: Try your local library for help or more information on the "how to" part of any of these opportunities if no company name is given.

Examples:

From the kitchen

Make cookies or candy. There are many success stories with these food products. Some businesses have remained small but very profitable, while others have grown from humble beginnings to become national companies. Keys to success include a novel product, good quality, and attractive packaging.

Dehydrate food. Here is a unique business that can be started with little experience or money. Dehydration removes moisture from food products so that they can be stored for long periods of time without refrigeration. To experiment, you can even use your kitchen oven if you leave the door slightly open to allow moisture to escape. You can purchase a small dehydrating oven for less than $100. The dehydrated food can be packaged in sealed plastic bags using inexpensive sealing equipment. Suggestions: Try selling to health-food and camping stores. General food stores may also be interested because many people prefer the natural flavor of these foods.

Make cheese. Here is an opportunity to provide fresh specialty cheeses to the customer who insists on quality. To start, most equipment can be found in your kitchen. For a catalog of cheesemaking books, cultures, and equipment, write the New England Cheesemaking Supply Company, 85 Main St., Ashfield, MA 01330.

Package food products. This is another area with many success stories. You buy products in large quantities and package them for retail sales. Edibles such as hard candies, nuts, and dried fruit can be packaged for holidays and special occasions. Another great opportunity is impulse items at tourist attractions and special events, such as fairs. If you are creative and artistic, you can easily develop a special package for edible items to suit each occasion.

Preparing food away from the kitchen

Make novelty foods. There are opportunities to provide special snack foods at fairs, sporting events, and outside schools. Foods include popcorn, doughnuts, candied apples, and shaved ice. Keep in mind that you will need to take both the equipment and ingredients to the site.

From the workshop

Make birdhouses or weather vanes. If you can develop some clever designs, there is an ongoing market for these items.

Make jigsaw puzzles. There are enough jigsaw puzzle fans to keep you busy for a long time if you show some creativity with the puzzles you make. Use interesting and unique pictures—the puzzle addicts love them. Also, there is an opportunity for custom-made puzzles.

Make fishing lures. If you are an avid fisherman, you know how much time and money the experts and would-like-to-be-experts spend on selecting lures. Hand-made lures have a special appeal. Suggestion: You may want to consider mail order in a number of magazines dedicated to or featuring fishing.

Make duck decoys. This is another popular item for the serious outdoorsman. Not only are decoys used for hunting, but quality decoys are often used as home decorations. If you are good at this, you can get top dollar for your work. Just pay attention to detail and accuracy.

Make bunk beds. People have made a nice living building bunk beds that they sell for prices well below what you would have to pay in a store. They have great appeal for children, including college students. Here is the address of a source for simple plans and some marketing ideas: Hadley's National Woodworkers Progress Association, 10 Commerce Drive, Mooresville, IN 46158.

Cast concrete lawn furniture and ornaments. Using inexpensive concrete, you can make a wide variety of rugged and attractive decorative pieces to decorate lawns. Some people design their own and then make wood patterns to cast the cement. Here is a company that offers many ready-made molds. They are not cheap, but they allow you to start quickly. Write to Concrete Machinery Company, Drawer 99, Hickory, NC 28603.

Print on T-shirts, caps, and bumper stickers. You may not be familiar with the silk-screen printing process. It is the simplest and least expensive way of printing, especially on larger articles. If you have any artistic or craft skills, this printing technique should be easy for you to learn. Then, all you need are some clever designs or slogans and you are in business. If you have a "hot item," you can sell and deliver to local stores almost overnight—a BIG advantage! For instruction books and supplies, try your local art store. For complete starter kits and supplies, write to Magic Systems, P.O. Box 23888, Tampa, FL 33623.

Embed items in plastic. People have made money embedding coins, flowers, even mustard seeds, in clear liquid plastic. The plastic then becomes rock-hard. You do not need much skill or equipment. Here are two companies you can contact Magic Systems, P.O. Box 23888, Tampa, FL 33623, or Castolite, 4915 Dean, Woodstock, IL 60098.

From the sewing room

Sew soft toys. There is a big opportunity for <u>safe</u> toys for small children. Stuffed toys can be sewn in the shape of dolls, animals, even trucks and airplanes, in just about any shape or color. If they are washable, all the better.

Sew stuffed animals. Though similar to soft toys just described, the difference is that these animals are usually sewn from fur-like fabric and appeal to kids of all ages. School mascots sell well to both high school and college students.

Sew quality aprons. The poor hostess. She is all dressed up but forced to spend time in the kitchen. With today's casual living, guests are likely to stroll into the kitchen. Here is where an attractive, quality apron would come in handy. Another possibility is to sew aprons for use at outdoor barbecues. These might be for men, so the design would be quite different from the woman's. Use your imagination to come up with clever designs.

Other opportunities

Package home products. This is similar to the packaging idea for foods listed earlier, but these products can be sold year-round. You buy the ingredients in volume, then package them in containers for retail sales. Products such as cleaning liquids, polishes, and hand creams can be sold this way. For product ideas, check your library for a book of chemical formulas for popular products. If you cannot buy ingredients and containers locally, look for the *Thomas Register of U.S. Manufacturers* at your local library.

Make craft items in quantity. Many people who started out making a number of different craft items have developed successful businesses by concentrating on producing quantities of just one or two items which they sell to stores. Examples include wood furniture, ceramics, jewelry, and sewn stuffed animals.

Package soil. More than one clever person has made good money selling soil from a state or foreign country. Native Texans will always be potential customers for a small bottle of "home," wherever they live. The same can be said for the millions of Americans with roots in a foreign country. Sometimes it can be part of history. For example, small pieces of the Berlin wall and sand from Desert Storm have been sold in this way. You have two challenges: first, getting a quantity of this "free" resource delivered to your home, and second, packaging it in a clever way.

C3 Production: Make to order

Description: You take orders for products and then make them. This can be further divided into two types:

- You take orders, then there is some time before you deliver the product. You may be able to buy parts and materials after you have an order.
- You make the product as people wait—for example, keys. Therefore, you have to have parts and materials on hand.

Concerns: Can you make enough products to meet the demand and give you the income you want?

Do you have a way to sell your output?

Can you make products in time to meet your customer's needs?

Tips: For opportunities that do not have a company listed, try your local library for information on the "how to" part of the opportunity.

Review Catalog C2, covering products you can make in advance. Properly marketed, some of these products can also be made to order, eliminating the need for you to build inventory in advance. However, you will need samples of your work to demonstrate the quality and look of your products.

Examples:

From the kitchen

Bake cakes and pies. You can try this if you are a very good baker with some outstanding recipes. Contact local restaurants or specialty food shops with samples of your best creations. Also, advertise to bake and decorate cakes for special occasions, such as birthdays, Valentine's Day, and Christmas.

Catering. Are you that great cook with unique and delicious recipes for appetizers and meals? Let people know you are in business so they can order your goodies for special occasions and parties.

Catering on site. This is a variation of standard catering. The big difference is that you buy the ingredients, prepare the meal in your client's home (except for pre-prepared appetizers or desserts), then serve it along with appropriate wines. It is best done by two people dressed in proper attire. Kitchen cleanup may be included. Several couples could get together to enjoy this elegant alternative to going to a restaurant. For a course on catering, contact International Correspondence Schools, 925 Oak Street, Scranton, PA 18515.

Prepare and deliver meals. There are people who live alone who have difficulty preparing a complete and nutritional meal. You can set up a service to take one-time orders, or arrange to deliver meals every day. Incidentally, there is also an opportunity for delivering meals to people who would rather not cook.

Snack packages for college students or military personnel. Do you live near a college or military base? Send a sales letter to parents and other relatives describing a number of "goodie" packages you can make up and deliver to the students or military relatives. For example, birthday cakes, special occasion gift baskets, or exam survival kits, to name just a few? The advantages you offer are providing fresh fruit, snacks, and bakery items that cannot be easily shipped from home, AND convenient shopping for parents, relatives, and friends.

From the workshop

Make custom birdhouses or weather vanes. If you can develop some clever designs, there is an excellent market for these items. They can be built and decorated to satisfy your customer's special request.

Make custom mail boxes. If you look around an area with single family homes, you will see that most homes, even expensive ones, have standard metal mailboxes. Here is a chance to offer custom mail boxes to match the home's design and the owner's taste.

Make custom jigsaw puzzles. Jigsaw puzzle enthusiasts are always looking for something different. You can meet that need by making custom puzzles using pictures or photos that would appeal to the enthusiast. These make great gifts!

Other workshop opportunities. Design and make to order:

Picture frames
Window boxes
Dog houses

From the sewing room

Sew or knit clothes to order. Have you noticed this trend in many dress shops these days? You find a dress you like only to find out there is a full rack of the same dress. Women like to have something that is in style and yet unique without spending a fortune. Here is an opportunity if you are clever and capable with a sewing machine or knitting needles. For a course on dressmaking and design, contact International Correspondence Schools, 925 Oak Street, Scranton, PA 18515.

Sew costumes. There are several opportunities for costumes. These include theater productions, and shops that rent costumes for events such as Halloween and costume parties. You should have the skills necessary to size patterns and work quickly to put the outfit together. The ability to design clever and original outfits could help you build a large customer base.

Make for businesses

Make custom carrying cases. There is an on-going market for carrying cases that are made to carry specific items, such as salesmen's samples and musical instruments. All that is required are some basic tools and certain materials and supplies. For a complete instruction course, contact Custom Case Supply Company, 6075 De Soto Avenue, Woodland Hills, CA 91365.

Imprint advertising specialties. One of the most effective but inexpensive ways that companies can advertise is by giving away free items imprinted with their name and advertising messages. Popular items include pens, pencils, and calendars. The following companies offer imprinting or small printing equipment: Business Advertising Specialties Corp., 9351 De Soto Avenue, Chatsworth, CA 91311, or Magic Systems, P.O. Box 23888, Tampa, FL 33623.

Other opportunities

Make "3-D" pictures. Here is a very simple idea that is becoming popular. Take a 6 to 9 inch photo of one or several persons and bond it to a rigid backing, such as plywood or other wood up to 3/4 inch thick. Then cut out the outline using a jigsaw. The result is a unique conversation piece that can be displayed at work or home. If you use thin plywood or plastic, you will have to make a stand to support the picture. If you use thicker wood, the picture may stand by itself.

Bronze baby shoes and other items. Here is a business that has been going for years. It involves taking baby shoes or other family mementos that people would like to save and plating them with real metal so that they can be exhibited for years. Every detail of the original item is kept. For more on this interesting and easy-to-learn business, here are two companies that offer complete programs of instruction and materials: Nichols Bronze Supply Co., 10555 U.S. Highway 98, P.O. Box 1904, Sebring, FL 33870, or United Bronze Plating, 181 Greenwood Avenue, Rumford, RI 02916. If you prefer a manual on electroplating, write to A-1 Printing, P.O. Box 2222, Waldorf, MD 20604.

Make PVC furniture. Poly-Vinyl Chloride (PVC) is a rugged plastic with many uses, including pipes for plumbing. Since it can withstand bad weather and moisture, it is an ideal material for outdoor and casual furniture. It takes very little equipment and materials to get started in this business. For full instructions and sources for materials, contact Available Plastics, P.O. Box 924, Huntsville, AL 35804.

Make craft items to order. Almost any craft item is enhanced when it is custom made or decorated to the buyer's wishes. Personalized items find ready buyers and make thoughtful gifts. The opportunities are endless since people love to see their names in print.

"While-you-wait" custom-made products

Unlike most of the items described so far in this segment, there are many products that can be made while your customer waits. This suggests a different way of working than described for the other items, where materials can be purchased after you have an order, reducing inventory expenses. With these new items, you must have all materials on hand to provide quick service. Therefore, you must invest in some inventory before you sell. However, here are some unique opportunities that can be started on a relatively small budget:

Make badge pins. These pin-on badges come in various sizes. They can be custom made quickly with a variety of sayings. Some can even be made with instant photos. All you need is a good imagination and one of the kits you can purchase from one of these three companies: Badge-A-Minit, 348 N. 30th Road, LaSalle, IL 61301, or Mr. Button, P.O. Box 68359, Indianapolis, IN 46268, or Polaroid Corporation, 575 Technology Square, Cambridge, MA 02139.

Package gifts in tin cans. Here's a wild one. With some special equipment, you can lock small gifts in a tin can. To complete the fun, select a label from a number of attractive designs. Then, the person receiving the gift must use a can opener to get to the gift, as you would with any canned goods. For more information, contact N.B. Nelson, P.O. Box 999, Whitefish Mountain, MT 59937.

Make embossed metal tags. With the device from this company, you can quickly emboss a wide variety of personalized metal tags. Contact Perma Products, 275 N.E. 166 Street, Miami, FL 33162.

Make custom license plates and bumper stickers. These are great impulse items for flea markets and fairs. The letters and emblems on the license plates are raised just like on a real license. The bumper stickers are quickly printed using an inexpensive device. For information, contact Magic Systems, P.O. Box 23888, Tampa, FL 33623.

Make personalized beaded products. Make bracelets and necklaces by stringing beads that spell the customer's name. Each bead has one letter imprinted on it so that a name can be quickly put together by selecting the proper beads. Beads come in a variety of colors. For complete startup kits, here are two companies you can contact: American Name Jewelry, 4407 Vineland Road, Suite D-5, Orlando, FL 32811, and Name Station, Suite 7, 200 Rittenhouse Circle North, Bristol, PA 19007.

If people knew how hard I had to work to gain mastery, it would not seem so wonderful at all - Michelangelo

C4 Production: Publish and sell information

Description: You write something—a book, a report, a manual—you have it printed, then you sell it.

This is one of the most active areas for people who want to be on their own—and fortunes have been made in the process. It can be a very rewarding and gratifying business. This is the information age, and people are willing to pay for information they need.

Concerns: Can you make enough products to meet the demand and give you the income you want?

Do you have a way to market your products?

Can you afford the printing costs?

Can you manage and afford the inventory of unsold products?

Unfortunately, too many people who are selling information are preying on the needs of the public by selling questionable information at inflated prices. Get-rich-quick schemes are the most frequent rip-offs and are a huge industry all by themselves. Others include 2 to 40 page "reports" promising cures for all types of financial problems. These reports are sold for up to $20, and more. With millions of Americans in a financial bind, you can see the opportunity. Personally, I have always stayed away from this type of activity—it is an individual choice that each person has to make.

Tips: You can publish a fairly simple report or booklet within the dollar limits set in this book. However, publishing a book yourself will take thousands of dollars.

There are several good books on the subject of self-publishing. Three of the best were written by people who practice what they preach and self-publish their own top-quality books and reports. Get their catalogs by writing:

John Kremer, Ad-Lib Publications, 51 N. Fifth Street, Fairfield, IA 52556

Dr. Jeffrey Lant, 50 Follen Street, Suite 507, Cambridge, MA 02138

Dan Poynter, Para Publishing, P.O. Box 4232, Santa Barbara, CA 93140

Examples

Information reports and books. To describe all aspects of selling information reports would take a separate book. As a simple overview, it works this way:

- You need to have a solution to a problem—or know something that many other people would also like to know. If you have the information, you can proceed to the next step. If you do not, you need to research the subject.

- Write it down. The length of the "report" might range from a single page to a book with hundreds of pages. Most run from 4 to 64 pages. Use a typewriter that produces quality printing, or better, a word processor with a laser printer. You want to use those originals as masters to print as many copies as you need.

- Have the copies printed. In most cases, you can use a local "quick-print" shop. If it is a fairly short report, sheets can be stapled together.

- Sell it. Mail order is by far the most frequently used way to sell information (see Catalog C9).

- The success of your product will be based on

  The number of people who have the problem you are writing about or want the information you are offering.

  How much they would be willing to pay for the information.

  How you tell people about (advertise) your report or book.

Publish a newsletter. If you have a strong interest in a subject and do not mind working against continuous deadlines, you might consider publishing a newsletter. Most of the points I mentioned above apply here as well. In addition, you have to set a publishing schedule, say monthly, then keep to it. Finding fresh information to fill from 4 to 8 pages every month can be a chore. On the other hand, the steady income from present and new subscribers can be a wonderful incentive. As an example, medical schools and clinics have discovered this opportunity to raise additional money. Today's health-conscious public is eagerly subscribing to medical newsletters on a variety of health topics.

The range of subjects for a newsletter is endless. Besides medicine, there are newsletters on financial advice, retirement, the environment, hobbies, sports, and music, to name just a few. Subscriptions range from \$10 to \$20 a year for most subjects, but up to \$100 for financial advice. In addition, there are dozens of newsletters catering to the business world, from the starting entrepreneur to the large corporation. These subscriptions can cost up to \$1000 and more.

Sell recipes. This is another form of selling information. If you look in the classified advertising sections of many magazines and supermarket weeklies such as the *National Enquirer*, you can see numerous ads for people selling their favorite recipes. Typically, one to ten recipes are sold for \$2 to \$5. Read these ads, see how people advertise, then order a few to see what you get for your money. Most will include offers selling you more recipes. You probably won't get rich, but if your offering has a wide appeal, you can make some good pocket money. While printing costs will be minimal, you will have to spend from a few dollars up to as much as \$100 for a classified advertisement, depending on the number of readers of the publication.

Publish a booklet about your town or neighborhood. These could take different forms, depending on who you expect your readers to be. If many tourists or business visitors come to your area, the booklet can be oriented toward describing local history, sights, attractions, and restaurants. If your area is residential, you can concentrate on describing local history and available business services. You can consider selling advertisements to be printed in the booklet to defray its cost. With enough ads, booklets could be distributed free, get wide circulation, and give you a nice profit.

Sell your computer programs as shareware. Have you written a program for a personal computer? If you believe that it is good enough so that others may want to use it, why not try to sell it? It could be a business program, a teaching program, graphics, or even a game. The big problem is trying to market your program, and shareware is a good solution.

Here is how it works. You submit your program to a company that advertises and distributes shareware. If the company likes your program, it will include it in its catalog, which is sent to many thousands of users of personal computers. Financial arrangements vary, but quite often you do not have to pay for the catalog listing. The shareware company makes its money by selling its customers working copies of programs for a very low fee—often $2 to $5 per diskette. In this way, customers get to try a program for a few dollars.

If a customer likes your program and decides to use it, he or she registers with you for a charge you establish, usually $15 to $100. The charge depends on the complexity of your program and the support you commit to provide. Support can include providing improvements you make to the program, manuals, and answering installation and technical questions.

Here are several companies that distribute shareware. Write for information on how to submit your programs for consideration:

People's Choice, 235 Germantown Bend Cove #1, Cordova, TN 38018

Software Excitement, P.O. Box 3072, 6475 Crater Lake Hwy., Central Point, OR 97502

The Software Labs, 3767 Overland Ave. #112-115, Los Angeles, CA 90034

Possibly the greatest source of human happiness is personal achievement - Herbert Hoover

C5 Production: Raise to sell

Description: You sell animals that you breed, or plants and produce that you grow. While there are major differences from the other "Production" opportunities, there are many business problems in common.

Concerns: Do you have the proper space and environment to keep animals or plants?

Are there local codes prohibiting these activities?

Do you have a way to sell your output?

Tips: Try your local library for information on the "how to" part of any of these opportunities. Other sources include the U.S. government or your state Department of Agriculture, or veterinary and agricultural departments of local colleges.

Examples:

Raise animals

Breed pedigree dogs or cats. If you have an interest in pedigree animals, and know your business, there are excellent opportunities to sell them. Entering your best animals at local shows can be both fun and profitable. (Attending important regional and national shows takes a great deal of time and money.) To learn more about raising show dogs, read the book *The Road to Westminister*, by Robert and Toni Freeman, published by Betterway Publications, P.O. Box 219, Crozet, VA 22932.

Other opportunities. Dogs, cats, and farm animals are only the beginning of a long list of living creatures you can raise for profit. Here are some others that have been successfully sold by resourceful people:

Sold to pet stores

Turtles
White mice
Tropical fish—many varieties
Golden hamsters
Sea horses

Sold to research laboratories

White mice
Guinea pigs
Golden hamsters

Sold to organic farmers

Ladybugs—to help eliminate pesky garden insects.

Sold for their fur

Mink

Sold to fishermen

Earthworms
Crickets
Minnows

Sold to zoos

Endangered animals. Most of us are aware that there are many species of animals in danger of becoming extinct. The plight of the bald eagle has been publicized for several years. The conscious efforts of many dedicated people have helped to increase the number of these birds, but it takes time. If you are an animal lover, there is a way you can help. You can raise smaller endangered animals right in your home—even in an apartment. Not only will you be aiding these animals, but you can also make some easy money. For further information, contact Zoovival, P.O. Box 15007, Clearwater, FL 34629.

Not sold, but raised for other purposes

Bees—for their honey
Angora rabbits—for their long, wool-like fur

Grow crops

In every country in the world, including the U.S., many people make all or part of their income from garden and farm products. They are sold in one of five ways: to stores, to food processors, at markets, from home stands, and by mail order. Beside the normal fruits and vegetables that people grow for profit, here are some new ideas to consider. Most can be grown in a small area. An excellent book showing how to get the most from even the smallest lot is *Cash From Square Foot Gardening*, by Mel Bartholomew, published by Rodale Press, 33 E. Minor St., Emmeus, PA 18098. For a manual that discusses many of the opportunities listed below contact Homestead Design, Inc., P.O. Box 1058 Bellingham, WA 98227.

Herbs. There are several attractive reasons for growing herbs. They are easy to grow. They do not require much growing space. There is a growing demand from consumers. A few of the more popular herbs are mint, basil, thyme, fennel, chives, and parsley. Look for the book *Profits From Your Backyard Herb Garden*, by Lee Sturdivant, published by San Juan Naturals, P.O. Box 642, Friday Harbor, WA 98250.

Soybean sprouts. Here is another very popular and easy-to-grow food plant. What makes soybean sprouts unique is that they grow from a bean to a saleable food in days, and they need little attention or special growing environment. In fact, some people grow them in their basements.

Special flowers. Some attractive and interesting plants are fairly easy to grow, even indoors. Such flowers include Gloxinias, African Violets, and many others. If you have a "green thumb" and room for plants, you might consider this opportunity. An interesting manual which explains how to grow many plants by propagation (cutting up one plant) can be obtained from Growbiz, P.O. Box 306, Seminary, MS 39479.

Bonsai trees. While this is a fascinating opportunity, it is not for someone in a hurry. Before you will have any marketable products, it could take several years and a good deal of patience. Bonsai is the Japanese art of growing mature trees that are one to two feet in height by cutting back on the root system. After you read up on the subject, you may be able to find dwarf trees in nature that can speed up the process by getting you started with older plants than you normally would use to start.

In the end, you may have some beautiful miniatures that can be sold for hundreds of dollars. I guarantee you will not want to sell them all!

My interest is in the future because I am going to spend the rest of my life there - Charles Kettering

C6 Production: Contract work

Description: You work at home assembling or finishing work supplied to you by companies. You return the finished products to the company, which then sells them. You are not an employee of the company, but operate as an independent contractor. You get paid for each assembled product you send back.

This type of work takes two forms:

1. You work with a local company. You are responsible for picking up the parts from the company and returning completed items. The company pays you a fixed amount for each item you assemble. Hence, the term "piece work."

   In a variation that is rapidly growing, you use a personal computer with a modem to send written information to the company over telephone lines.

2. You work by mail with a company outside of your area. The company mails you a "starter kit" of components which you buy for $25 to $50. You assemble the components and ship them back to the company. The company then pays you a fixed amount for each completed item you return. Many of these programs involve assembling or decorating items, or sewing.

   "Envelope stuffing" is another form of this activity. A company sends you envelopes, printed material, and a list of names. You fold and insert (stuff) the printed material into the envelope, then address, stamp and mail the envelopes.

Concerns: Home assembly work for other companies may be restricted in your state or city. Many of these laws were enacted years ago to protect home workers from safety violations and to prevent minimum wage abuses. Check with your state labor department before getting involved with a company.

Check to be sure you are not violating local zoning regulations. See Lesson 24 for more on this.

Warning: Unfortunately, there are many companies offering questionable mail programs for home assembly work and envelope stuffing. Many of these companies make their money from the starter kits you must buy.

If you are concerned that you might lose your money, I recommend you carefully study a company and its products before committing to participate in its program. Contact the Better Business Bureau in the city where the company has its main office.

You can write the company and ask for names and addresses of people in its program that you can contact. If it will not provide names, I suggest you look for a different opportunity. If it does provide names, contact those people and ask questions such as the following:

How long have they been with the program?

Is the program what they expected?

How does the company handle rejects?

How quickly does the company pay?

Tips: If possible, work with a local company. This avoids the problems of working through the mail and gives you a chance to meet and know the people you are working with.

There are companies that offer homework for people who live nearby. There are several ways to look for these companies, including employment agencies, help-wanted advertisements, and personally contacting local companies. An excellent book covering many aspects of working from home and listing over 1,000 job opportunities is *The Work-at-Home Sourcebook*, by Lynie Arden, published by Live Oak Publications, P.O. Box 2193, Boulder, Colorado 80306.

C7 Sales: Buy to sell

Description: You buy products and then sell them. This means you will have to have inventory on hand.

Concerns: Check with the supplying company to see if it has a minimum dollar amount you must spend when you order. If so, can you manage this expense?

Can you manage and afford an inventory of unsold products?

Do you have a way to sell your products?

If displays or sales aids are required, can you afford quality items that will attract buyers?

Tips: If you are interested in sales, make sure you also review the next segment, Catalog C8, which describes sales opportunities where you normally do not buy products in advance. However, if you wanted to, you could buy some of those products in advance so you can give the customer the product when you make the sale. It depends on how you intend to sell. If you plan to sell and deliver at the same time (as at a fair or mall), then you must have the merchandise available to give to the customer. If you can show samples and take orders for later delivery, you can save money by not having inventory expenses.

Get started with one product line. As you learn and grow, you can add additional lines. When you are ready to grow, see Lesson 37 for suggestions.

Examples by product type

There are thousands of sources for products that you may want to sell. I describe how to find sources in Lesson 30. You may have difficulty in buying from some large companies which only ship big volumes to established businesses. But here is a sampling of companies which are interested in having people like you sell their products. They offer opportunities that can be started with less than $100 to several hundred dollars. Write to any of these companies for information on their products.

Jewelry

Here are companies that you can contact to purchase inexpensive jewelry at very low prices. Most will send you a catalog on request, and will sell you samples and a starter kit. I have noted company specialties, if appropriate.

Bosco Jewelers, Inc. P.O. Box 8426, Albuquerque, NM 87198	Turquoise and sterling silver
Fireside Treasures 924 E. Maynard Road, Cary, NC 27511	Rings, pins, bracelets
Judee K Creations, Inc. 13330 Bessemer Street, Van Nuys, CA 91401	Gold and silver chains by the inch, jewelry
Lasting Impressions, Inc. Box 22065, Lake Buena Vista, FL 32830	Gold, silver, jeweled chains by the inch, jewelry
Merlite Industries, Inc. 114 Fifth Avenue, New York, NY 10011	Rings, chains, etc.
Navajo Manufacturing Company 5801 Logan Street, Denver, CO 80216	Turquoise and sterling silver, novelties
Richmond Sales, Inc. 42 Power Road, Pawtucket, RI 02860	Inexpensive jewelry
U.S. Gold Manufacturing Co. 11460 N. Cave Creek Road, Phoenix, AZ 85020	Gold chain by the inch, jewelry

Personal protection products

This is a rapidly growing opportunity. People are looking for low-cost and effective devices for protection against muggers and other criminals. Please note that some states and cities have ordinances against the use of such devices, particularly sprays. Others require a permit to use them. Check with local authorities, such as the police, before deciding to spend any money or time on this.

Assault-Gard Securities Products — Self-defense sprays and battery stun devices
10255 E. 25th Ave., Suite 8, Aurora, CO 80010

Chrysler Chemical Co. — Self-defense sprays
P.O. Box 335, Hewlett, NY 11557

Gard-a-Car, Inc. — Car anti-theft devices
8143 Macomb, P.O. Box 294, Grosse Ile, MI 48138

Hankins Marketing Corporation — Self-defense sprays
128 N. Merritt Ave., P.O. Box 1681, Salisbury, NC 28144

United Defense Industries, Inc. — Self-defense sprays
205 West Deer Valley Road, Phoenix, AZ 85027

Other novel opportunities

Here is a variety of other product ideas you can pursue. Some are serious, and others are fun. All have the potential to make you money. You should pick product lines with which you are comfortable.

Astrascope Corporation — Monthly astrology charts
78 Stone Place, Melrose, MA 02176

Chemical Light, Inc. — Night glow and battery-lit products
505 Harvester, Wheeling, IL 60090

Dreamscapes — Shifting sand pictures and holograms
2140 E. 7th Place #1, Los Angeles, CA 90021

EA of Hawaii — Hawaiian design quilts and pillows
733 Bishop Street, Suite 170-114, Honolulu, HI 96813

Exotic Tropical Seeds — Seeds to grow exotic tropical plants
9401-66 Place North, Brooklyn Park, MN 55428

Franz Sign Company — Ready-made business signs
8 Glover Street, Portsmouth, OH 45662

Future Thunder Productions — Flying stunt toy planes
245 E. 63rd Street, Suite 612, New York, NY 10021

International Polymer — Cleaner, polisher, sealer liquids
3398 Sanford Drive, Marietta, GA 30066

Kidco Products, Inc. 917-5 Lincoln Avenue, Holbrook, NY 11741	Stuffed toy animals
National Stock Sign Company P.O. Box 145, Santa Cruz, CA 95063	Ready-made business signs
Pandora's Plus P. O. Box 40434, Fayetteville, NC 28309	Inexpensive copies of name perfumes
Pick Point Enterprises, Inc. P.O. Box 220, Mirror Lake, NH 03853	Night-glow balls, lures, etc.
Sentique Perfume - USA 4471 W. 160th Street, Cleveland, OH 44135	Inexpensive copies of name perfumes

Vending machines

Servicing a number of installed vending machines can provide good income. However, there is only a limited opportunity if you want to stay within the dollar limits of this book. Most vending machines are expensive. They have to be to assure rugged construction and reliability. However, there are some inexpensive machines that will dispense smaller candies and nuts. If you are willing to start small, with limited income, you can "plow back" your profits to buy additional machines. You will not get rich, but over time you can have a growing income with very little work. Contact:

Haymco Marketing, 130 W. Hampton, Suite 4, Mesa, AZ 85210

Parkway Machine Corp., 1930 Greenspring Drive, Timonium, MD 21093

Vendall Marketing Corp., 1150 Knutson, Medford, OR 97504

Here is another vending machine opportunity. Many companies have vending machines installed for their employees to use. Quite often the companies use a vending service, which provides the machines and keeps them stocked. You can offer companies an alternative by offering to sell them machines they stock themselves. These machines are more expensive than those described above, but you do not have to buy them. You get paid a commission on machines you sell. Contact:

Federal Machine Corp., P.O. Box 1779, Des Moines, IA 50306

The person who makes a success of living is the one who sees his goal steadily and aims for it unswervingly - Cecil B. de Mille

C8 Sales: Sell to order

Description: First, you take orders for products—the customer gets the products at a later time. You act as an agent or a "middleman" between your customers and your supplier.

Products are delivered in one of three ways:

- You buy from suppliers at wholesale prices. They ship products to you to deliver to the customer. The customer pays you the retail price.
- You get paid the retail price by the customer. You pay the supplier a wholesale price. The supplier then ships the products directly to your customers. This is known as drop-shipping, and is frequently used with mail order or when buying large items.
- You take orders and send them to the supplier. The supplier ships to your customer, who then pays the supplier the retail price. The supplier pays you a commission, or the dollar amount between retail and wholesale prices.

In all three cases, you will not need to have inventory on hand. However, in most cases you will have to buy samples so that potential customers can see the products for themselves. Sometimes, catalogs and descriptive brochures can be used in place of actual products.

Concerns: Do you have a way to sell your products?

With some of the companies listed in this segment, you can start with no investment. Other companies require an initial fee to buy samples or a starter kit. Your investment could be from $25 to $700, depending on the company and program. If you must make an investment, be sure you understand your commitment before you get involved.

If you do not have actual products, do you have good descriptive sales aids to show customers so that they will buy without actually seeing your products?

If displays or sales aids are required, can you afford quality materials that will attract buyers?

Tips: If you are interested in sales, make sure you also review the previous segment, Catalog C7, which describes sales opportunities where you pay for and stock merchandise before you sell it. You may not want to spend money up front—it depends on how you intend to sell. If you plan to sell and deliver at the same time (as at a fair or mall), then you must have the merchandise available to give to the customer. If you can show samples or brochures and take orders for later delivery, you can save money by not having inventory expenses.

Get started with one product line. As you learn and grow, you can add additional lines. When you are ready to grow, see Lesson 37 for suggestions.

Examples by product type

There are thousands of sources for products that you may want to sell. I describe how to find sources in Lesson 30. You may have difficulty in buying from some large companies which only ship big volumes to established companies. But here is a sampling of companies which are interested in selling through people who want to get started. They offer opportunities that can be started with little or no money. Write to any of these companies for information on their products.

The opportunities in this segment are divided into two parts. The first part describes sales opportunities with consumer and home products. The second part discusses opportunities to sell to businesses.

Selling consumer and home products

Jewelry

Face Your Colors 68 Little Briggins, Fairport, NY 14450	Colored jewelry and color consultants

Look-a-Likes — Zirconium jewelry
1695 Barbara Lane, East Meadow, NY 11554

Lady Remington Fashion Jewelry — Fashion jewelry
818 Thorndale Ave., Bensenville, IL 60106

Cosmetics and skin care

This is an area that has been one of the most active for independent business people for many years. Avon was one of the first companies, and is still the largest company selling these products. Here are a few companies looking for independent agents.

Avon Products, Inc. — Cosmetics, jewelry, clothing
Nine W. 57th Street, New York, NY 10091

Concepts Now Cosmetics — Cosmetics and skin care
10200 Pioneer Blvd., Santa Fe Springs, CA 90670

Lumé International — Nail hardeners and conditioners
6132 S. 380 W., P.O. Box 57910, Salt Lake City, UT 84157

Mary Kay Cosmetics, Inc. — Cosmetics and skin care
8787-T Stemmons Frwy., Dallas, TX 75247

Nu Skin International, Inc. — Cosmetics and skin care
P.O. Box 801, Provo, UT 84603

Orifame, International — Cosmetics and skin care
76 Treble Cove Rd., N. Billerica, MA 01862

Women's apparel

Today, there are more women working, so there is less time for them to shop. These companies offer apparel which can be sold in a number of ways, such as house parties or by appointment:

A & E Apparel, Inc. — Knit fashions
2636 Walnut Hill Lane, Suite 205, Dallas, TX 75229

Doncaster — Women's better apparel
P.O. Box 1159, Oak Springs Rd., Rutherfordton, NC 28139

Satin Doll Enterprises — Lingerie
78 Water St., Beverly, MA 01915

Men's shoes

Here are two well established companies that offer full lines of men's shoes:

Hanover Shoe Co.
Direct Sales, 118 Carlisle St., Hanover, PA 17331

Mason Shoe Manufacturing Company
Chippewa Falls, WI 54774

Health products

This is another endless opportunity. People want to look and feel their best. These companies say they can help:

Shaklee U.S., Inc. — Vitamins, diet products, cosmetics, cleaners
151 Docks Corner Rd., Dayton, NJ 08810

Vitamin Power — Vitamin catalogs with your name imprinted
P.O. Box 3037, 39 St. Mary's Place, Freeport, NY 11520

United American Marketing, Inc. — Customized diet programs
27280 Haggerty Rd., C-14, Farmington Hills, MI 48331

Uni-vite, Inc. — Diet programs
2440 Impala Drive, Carlsbad, CA 92008

Home products

This is the grand-daddy of opportunities for people who want to sell products while staying independent. Originally, most sales were made door-to-door. Products included brushes, vacuum cleaners, and encyclopedias. Today, both the products and sales techniques have changed considerably. Take a look:

Amway Corporation — Cleaning products, vitamins, jewelry
7575 E. Fulton Road, Ada, MI 49355

Hurley Chicago Co., Inc. — Water purifiers
12621 S. Laramie Ave., Alsip, IL 60658

Kitchen Fair — Kitchen cookware and accessories
1090 Redmond Road, Jacksonville, AR 72076

Multi-Pure Drinking Water Systems 21339 Nordhoff St., Chatsworth, CA 91311	Water purifiers
Nationwide Carpet Brokers P.O. Box 1472, Dalton, GA 30722	Discount carpeting
Transworld Industries 2961 W. Glenlord Rd., Stevensville, MI 49127	Water filters and beauty aids
Tupperware Company P.O. Box 2353, Orlando, FL 32802	Plastic kitchen products

Gift items and general merchandise

This is a wide area, covering items from small novelties to crystal and TV sets. The following companies will provide you with attractive catalogs of the products they can provide you. Many of the companies will drop-ship for you.

B & F Systems P.O. Box 660036, Dallas, TX 75266	Selected general merchandise
Cook Bros., Inc. 240 N. Ashland Ave., Chicago, IL 60607	General merchandise
Grant Park Gifts E1217 13th, Spokane, WA 99202	Gifts and novelty items
Princess House, Inc. 455 Somerset Ave., North Dighton, MA 02754	Giftware and home products
Strawser Specialty Company 1318 S. Finley Rd., Lombard, IL 60148	Giftware and home products
Specialty Merchandise Corp. 9401 DeSoto Ave., Chatsworth, CA 91311	General merchandise

Greeting and special cards

Cards can be sold in a number of ways. They can be sold to individuals as well as to stores. The following companies also offer stationery and novelty products to complement their card lines.

Carlson Craft
P.O. Box 8700, North Mankato, MN 56002

Creative Card Company
4401 W. Cermak Rd., Chicago, IL 60623

Moderne Card Company
3855 N. Lincoln Ave., Chicago, IL 60613

Other novel opportunities

Here are a few more companies with interesting products to offer:

Agency Bureau Hearst Magazines 250 W. 55th St., New York, NY 10019	Magazine subscriptions
Cradlegram Box 16-4135, Miami, FL 33116	Personalized baby announcements
Jeff Roberts Company 299 Newport Ave., Wollaston, MA 02170	Children's story books personalized with child's name and photos
Mind Communications, Inc. 1844 Porter St. S.W., P.O. Box 904, Wyoming, MI 49509	Distribute catalogs of subliminal tapes
Select Coupon Program 106 S. Central Ave., Elmsford, NY 10523	Discount coupon program memberships
Zapper 1 Antenna Systems 7923 Floyd St., Suite 449, Overland Park, KS 66204	Small dish TV satellite antennas

Selling to businesses

Manufacturers' representative (Rep.)

If you have business sales experience, you can contact companies around the country to see if you can represent them in your area. Many companies cannot afford to have their own sales people in all parts of the country. You are not an employee of the company, but you get orders from your customers and send the orders to the company. The company takes care of all billing, shipments, and payments. You get a commission on the sales you make. If you can represent several non-competing companies in your area, you can make an excellent living. If you would like to join an association which will provide helpful information and contacts, write to United Association Manufacturers' Representatives, 113 Terrace Trail West, Lake Quivira, KS 66106.

Products for business

If you prefer to sell to businesses, there are numerous opportunities. In some cases, you conduct your business the same as a manufacturers' rep.. In other cases, you buy the products or supplies from the manufacturer at wholesale. Then you bill the customer full price under your own company name. Here are some companies who depend on people like you to sell their products:

AM Marketing 694 Center Street, Chicopee, MA 01013	Business cards with photos
Authentiprint 258 'A' St., P.O. Box 1349, Ashland, OR 97520	Thumb print recorder for check cashing
Business Advertising Specialties Corp. 9351 DeSoto Ave., Chatsworth, CA 91311	Imprinted advertising specialties
Blimpie Floating Signs 6292 Windlass Circle, Boynton Beach, FL 33437	Huge inflated advertising balloons
Catalyst Communications Corp. 146 S. Atlantic Ave., Ormond Beach, FL 32176	Specialized telephone services
Colorfast Marketing Systems 9522 Topanga Canyon Blvd., Chatsworth, CA 91311	Business cards with photos
Divnick International, Inc. 1680 East Street, Spring Valley, OH 45370	Novel coin collectors for charities
Federal Machine Corp. P.O. Box 1779, Des Moines, IA 50306	Sell vending machines
Kaeser & Blair, Inc. 953 Martin Place, Cincinnati, OH 45202	Advertising specialties
Kustom Cards USA, Inc. 219 Walnut Ave., P.O. Box 590, Vinton, VA 24179	Business cards with photos
KC Business Forms Co. P.O. Box 128, Tecumseh, KS 66542	Custom printed business forms
Logo Watch Co. 44 E. Center, Logan, UT 84321	Watches, etc., with company logo

McGrew Color Graphics 1615 Grand Ave., P.O. Box 419716, Kansas City, MO 64141	Color printing (must have experience)
Photo Express 3572 Hancock Street, San Diego, CA 92110	Business cards with photos
Positive Concepts Ltd. 561 Thornton Rd., Lithia Springs, GA 30057	Business cards with photos
The Premium Connection 6275 Harrison, Suite 1, Las Vegas, NV 89120	Products for premiums and incentive plans
Research Marketing 7421 - 114th Ave. North, Suite 205, Largo, FL 34643	Talking messages near merchandise or displays
Surveillance Video Systems 258 'A' St., P.O. Box 1349, Ashland, OR 97520	Surveillance cameras for stores
Testrite Instrument Co., Inc. 135 Monroe Street, Newark, NJ 07105	Luminous signs for restaurants and bars
Valiant I.M.C. 195 Bonhomme St., P.O. Box 488, Hackensack, NJ 07602	Video and audio equipment
Visual Images 300 Richfield St., Suite 201, Pittsburgh, PA 15234	Business cards with photos

Whatever you can do or dream you can do, begin it.
Boldness has a genius, power and magic in it - Johann von Goethe

C9 Sales: Mail order

Description: You run a retail business from your home by shipping your products to customers through the mail. You can reach customers by advertising in a number of ways. Mail order gives you great flexibility in the hours you work.

Concerns: Before starting, do your homework! Take the time to learn about the business before committing a single dollar. Remember, one of the basic principles of this book is to start by spending time, not dollars.

At one time or another, almost everyone has thought about going into the mail-order business. The reasons? Besides the advantages mentioned above, everyone has heard the stories of overnight millionaires and easy living. And it all seems so simple!

These stories have been verified in some cases. However, there are many more cases that did not produce the desired results, often with a significant waste of time and money. Making money in mail order takes attention to detail. You definitely should not proceed until you know how and where to advertise to reach the people you want to buy your product. This may not be a simple matter.

Tips: Many successful mail-order operators make their money by placing small, inexpensive advertisements in many publications, rather than betting all their money on a few big, expensive ads.

To cover all the important aspects of mail order would require a full-length book, which is well beyond the space I can give here. If you want to learn more, there are several good books on the subject. If you want a thorough understanding, two of the best are:

How to Start and Operate a Mail Order Business, by Julien L. Simon, published by McGraw-Hill,

Building a Mail Order Business, by William A. Cohen, published by John Wiley & Sons.

Both Drs. Simon and Cohen are college professors with many years of practical experience in small businesses. Unlike many "get-rich-quick" books on mail order, these books do not take short cuts and they point out potential problem areas.

Packaged programs

Some companies offer training programs and all material necessary to get started, including catalogs printed with your company's name. If you wish, some will "drop ship" merchandise for you. You forward all orders for merchandise to them, and they ship the merchandise directly to your customer under your name. In this way, you eliminate the need to buy inventory, a major expense and headache.

I have heard both positive and negative stories about your chances of success using packaged programs. If you want to learn more, here are three companies that have been in the business for many years. If interested, contact them and make your own judgments.

The Mellinger Company, 6100 Variel Ave, Woodland Hills, CA 91367,

Mail Order Associates, 120 Chestnut Ridge Road, Montvale, NJ 07645,

SMC, 9401 DeSoto Avenue, Chatsworth, CA 91311.

A mail order short course

In no way is this "short course" intended to provide all the answers. Rather, it is meant to show you the many things that have to be done before you will have a successful business. Can it be done? Of course! Just be prepared to do your homework.

Picking a product

Although just about everything has been successfully sold by mail, here are some desirable features to consider when selecting a product:

- Select products that appeal to a wide range of people, but are not easy to find in local stores.

- Pick products that can be priced so that you make enough profit. If you are selling only one product, look for one that you can sell for $10 to $20. This should allow you to make a reasonable profit after all expenses.

- Look for products that will not break in shipment. Also, lighter weight products are less expensive to ship.

- Offer more than one product. If customers are pleased with their purchases, they will want to buy more from you. Repeat business is a very important strategy for making your company grow.

Sources for products

There are many approaches to finding a product that you would like to sell. See Lesson 30 for more on possible sources and how to approach them. Also, review Catalogs C7 and C8 for companies with products you may want to sell by mail order. If you are interested in selling books by mail, see the end of this segment.

Pricing

As a rough rule, if you buy a product for $3.50, you should sell it for $10 to $20. A "markup" of 3 to 1 should be as low as you should price, with 5 to 1 being safer. If you can get more, go for it! But make sure it will sell by testing (see below). Your markup will be influenced by a number of factors, including the price of your products, whether you are selling one or many different items, and what competition charges.

If you are completely unfamiliar with mail order, you may wonder why you need these markups. You must remember there are many expenses beyond the cost of the product. These include:

Advertising
Packaging and labeling
Postage
Returns
Bad checks
Overhead

Advertising

There are many ways you can reach potential customers. The traditional mail order approaches are as follows:

Catalogs. Mail catalogs to possible buyers. Creating your own catalog when you start would take a great deal more money than assumed in this book. But the companies with packaged programs mentioned earlier can provide you with catalogs.

Direct mail. Mail sales letters to possible customers.

Classified ads. Solicit business by placing small, inexpensive advertisements in the classified sections of magazines or newspapers. There are two basic approaches:

- You can try to make the sale directly with the advertisement. This will work if you can describe your product in a few words AND if it is priced fairly low, say up to $5. You may be able to price somewhat higher, depending on the product.

- Your ad can instruct the reader to send for free information. You would then send a detailed sales letter, usually 4 to 8 pages. If you are asking $10, $25, $50 or more for your product, customers must be assured that they are getting their money's worth. Your sales letter must provide that assurance.

Display ads. Place larger, more expensive ads in magazines or newspapers. These can vary from a small, 1-inch-high ad up to a full page.

Some more advanced ways to reach mail order customers include:

Telephone. Solicit business by making calls to prospects. You can make the calls yourself, or use automatic equipment with recordings.

Personal computer "bulletin boards." If you have a computer with a modem (ability to communicate with other PCs over telephone lines), you may be aware of bulletin boards provided by clubs and companies to support the exchange of PC information. Some people are using bulletin boards to advertise products such as PC programs and games.

Radio. You solicit business by advertising on radio. Most likely this will be beyond the dollar limits of this book. However, if you are determined, you may be able to persuade a local station to allow you a "per inquiry" agreement. Instead of a fixed charge, the station receives a portion of your profits on radio sales.

Television. You solicit business by advertising on television. This will be even more difficult for a newcomer to achieve within tight dollar constraints. You will need an interesting product and high-quality, professionally made advertisements. These can cost tens of thousands of dollars—even more!

A combination of two or more of these techniques. In most cases, you will find successful mail order operators using a combination of techniques. For example, you can place a classified ad in a magazine and have the prospect telephone a number to hear a recording. In turn, the recording would encourage the listener to send for further information.

Preparing your advertisement

This is one of the most critical steps in the mail order process. No matter how good your product is, your advertising can make or break its profitability. <u>You must take time to write even the simplest ad.</u> Once it is written, you must test its effectiveness before committing to a major campaign.

How you intend to advertise will influence how and what you will write. For example, if you intend to use classified ads, you must learn to make every word count. Classifieds are typically 10 to 25 words in length, and you pay for each word. On other hand, if you intend to use a direct mail approach and mail sales letters to prospects, you would write hundreds of words, explaining in detail the features and values of your products. For more specific advice on the various advertising approaches, I recommend the books by Simon and Cohen mentioned earlier under "tips."

When you write advertisements, use words that stress the value of your product to help the readers satisfy their needs. Make every word count.

<u>Attracting reader's attention</u> - there are certain subjects that cover the needs of a large number of readers. These include:

How to make money
Health issues and concerns
Losing weight

Security
Romance
Being accepted by others
Making life easier
Leisure-time activities

Study television commercials and magazine advertisements. They are written and coordinated by highly paid advertising experts. Notice how often they play on the needs listed above. Of greater importance, study mail-order advertisements. Go to your local library and review magazines with mail-order ads. Review older issues of those magazines and look for ads that are repeated month after month. Ads are expensive, and no smart mail-order operator would run an ad continuously unless it was making money!

Testing

Few businesses give you as many chances to test what you are doing as does mail order. This is good news because continuous testing should be an important part of your business. If you go into mail order, you must be constantly looking for ways to improve your business. Key areas you should be testing include:

- How are you spending your advertising dollars?

  Where are you placing your ads?

  What is the best size, layout, and wording for a particular ad?

- How effective are your ads in different magazines or newspapers? This is why "keying" ads is so important (see below).

- What is the best price for your product? Will raising or lowering your price actually give you more total profit? Here is how this could work. If you raise prices, you may not sell as many units, but you will be making more profit with each sale. Lowering prices could also bring in more money. Even though you make less money per sale, you will probably sell more units, bringing you more profit for the total program. If you think that this is an "always win" situation, keep in mind that in either case you will not make any profit unless you sell enough units.

The mail order campaign

Here is a summary of the steps you should take to sell by mail order. While your advertising method may be different, I will use magazine classified advertising to illustrate the steps.

1. Select a product or products.

2. Decide what advertising method (or methods) you will use—are you going to sell through magazine classifieds, direct mail,...?

3. Decide where you will advertise. Specifically, which magazines are you going to use? Base your selections on the types of readers of different magazines. For example, a fishing rod should be advertised in men's outdoor magazines, such as *Field and Stream*, or maybe *Popular Science*, not in *Vogue* or *Better Homes and Gardens*. For references which list all magazines published in the U.S., look for the following volumes at your local library: *Consumer Magazine and Agri-Media Rates & Data*, published monthly by Standard Rate & Data Service, Wilmette, IL, or the *Gale Directory of Publications and Broadcast Media*, published by Gale Research, Detroit, MI.

4. Write to the magazines you have selected and request a "rate card," which gives their advertising rates. The address of the advertising manager appears near the front of most magazines. Rates can also be found in the Standard Data & Rate Service volume, listed above. However, some rates could be out of date.

5. Prepare the advertisements.

6. "Key" ads so that orders can be traced to specific ads and dates. That is, add a code in your address, such as "Dept. 44." Use a different code for each magazine and month. The key will tell you from which ad each customer ordered.

7. Place (buy) advertisements in the selected magazines.

8. Receive orders and mail out products (order fulfillment).

9. Test, test, test.

    - Keep accurate records of the number of orders received from each advertisement.

    - Analyze sales results to determine which ads in which magazines created the most sales, and which ads should be changed or dropped.

- **Based on earlier results, place additional ads in the magazines that have had successful sales.**

- **Try changing words and layouts to make your ads more effective.**

- **Continue to key ads so that you can test the effectiveness of changes.**

Books: a unique product opportunity

If you are not sure of what products to sell, consider books. Many mail order booksellers specialize in a limited subject area. They know that once they build their customer list, many customers will continue to buy from them. Repeat business is key to long-term success in mail order.

While there are no major companies dominating the field, selling books by mail is big business. If you review the above list of desirable features for a mail-order product, you will see why. While books do not meet the criteria for light weight, there is a special U.S. mail classification (special fourth-class book rate) that can be used to ship inexpensively. However, delivery this way is slow, so you may want to charge more for "shipping and handling," and use U.S. mail first-class or United Parcel Service.

Two of the biggest areas of customer interest are making money and self-improvement. In fact, this opportunity is so big that there are many businesses making big money selling inferior products. Typically, the advertisements for these books promise all sorts of miracle results. Unfortunately, you cannot be sure of the quality of a book until you receive it. How do you know what to buy? If you deal with a name publisher, you probably will not have quality problems, but you could be competing with book stores selling the same book. Less-known suppliers could provide books that are not available in stores, but quality could be a question. If you decide to try book selling, my advice to you is to take your time selecting your supplier and every book you intend to sell.

Decide what type of books you want to sell. Then visit your local library and look through the 3-volume *Books in Print*, published by R.R. Bowker Co. Published annually, the volumes list all books currently in print. All legitimate publishers submit this information. Books are listed by both author and title, and information on publishers is provided. Contact those publishers you are interested in and ask for their latest catalogs.

C10 Sales: by MLM Multi-Level Marketing

Description: You represent companies with MLM programs—also known as Network Marketing—to make money in two ways:

> By selling the company's products as a distributor or agent. You get paid a commission on what you sell.
>
> By sponsoring other people to become distributors. You also get a commission on what they sell. In turn, the distributors you sponsored recruit others. You get a small commission on <u>all</u> their sales ("down-line" sales) as well.

The number of distributor "levels" varies among companies that sell through MLM. Often you will see four or five levels.

Concerns: Yes, there are cases where fortunes have been made. This usually requires you to get involved early with the right company and the right products, so that you can build a strong network that lasts for years. As examples, two well-known MLM companies, Shaklee and Amway, have many wealthy distributors.

WARNING: Stories of success have prompted some rather shady companies to appear. In one scheme, the company offers what appears to be a bona fide MLM program. However, it is little more than an illegal "pyramid" scheme. The strategy is to sell distributorships by charging a fee or requiring the purchase of large quantities of products. The company makes most of its money by selling distributorships, and its products are only used to accomplish this goal.

Tips: Before committing to any MLM program, you must decide if the program is a legitimate opportunity or a scam. Check out the MLM company and its products (see "Questions to ask," on the next page).

Assuming you are investigating a legitimate program, the best opportunity for you will depend on the type of person you are.

- In older, well-established companies, products and product quality are known. However, opportunities for rapid growth may be limited by some degree of saturation. This affects the number of sales you can make as well as your ability to find people you can sponsor to become distributors.

- Young companies may have more risk, but also may have the potential for greater rewards. The reputation and quality of their products may not be established and they could have problems with too rapid growth. However, there is more opportunity to sell a new product <u>and</u> to sponsor new distributors.

How they work

If you build a strong "network" of recruits with the <u>right</u> company, you can make big money. Look at this simple example. In addition to selling products, over time you sponsor three new distributors. They each sponsor three more, and in time the new distributors each sponsor three more. A simple diagram would look like this:

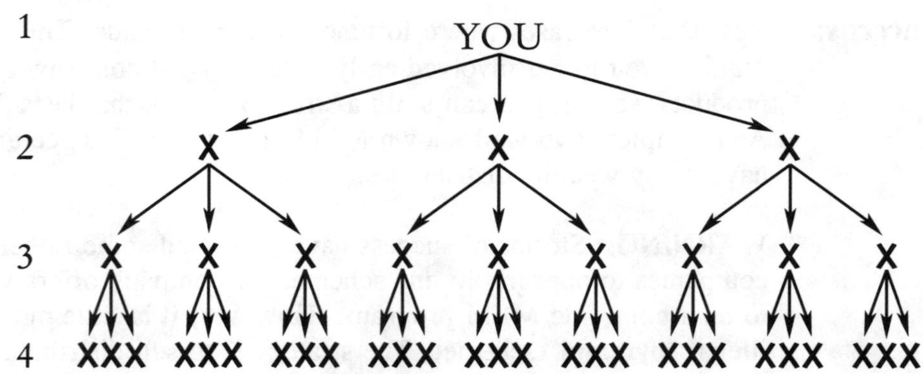

It would appear that you could be making money from the efforts of 39 other people and, with even more distributors, you could become rich. But remember—getting distributors may not be easy, and not all distributors will be productive. Although many people make a reasonable business from proven MLM programs, few become rich. Meanwhile, others are wasting time on questionable programs.

Questions to ask

Here are some questions to ask before you commit to a MLM program:

The company

How long has the company been in business?

What reputation does it have?

What type of growth is it experiencing?

Are sponsors selling products—or only recruiting new distributors?

Products

Are its products useful and of high quality?

Would you be proud to sell the company's products?

Service

What type of sales aids (brochures, samples, etc.) are available?

How does it get products to you and your customers?

How frequently and promptly does it pay commissions?

What system does it have to calculate commissions you receive from sales made by distributors you sponsored?

How does it handle returned products?

Your commitment

What type of investment will you have to make? (It should be relatively small.)

How much time are you expected to put into this work?

Summary

Keep your eyes open for legitimate opportunities. Check them out using the questions shown above. If everything looks good, pay particular attention to the age and growth record of the company. If growth is your goal, take a chance on a solid, rapidly growing company.

When you commit to a program, work hard at doing a thorough job. Attend sales meetings, make your sales, and keep looking for people whom you think would be good distributors.

When hopes are soaring, I always repeat to myself, two plus two make four, and no one has ever invented a way of getting something for nothing - Bernard Baruch

C11 Service: for individuals

Description: You provide a service (do something) for other people.

Concerns: Do you have a way to reach potential customers?

Do you have the expertise to provide the service?

Some businesses may require you to have a license or permit. See Lesson 23. Some may require extra insurance coverage.

Tip: To help others, you should project confidence and competence. Never commit to do something unless you are confident you can deliver.

Examples by type of service

There are thousands of known services you could provide, and probably many more still to be developed. We live in a changing world, and change brings opportunity.

I have divided these opportunities into five general categories: Professional, Caring, Instructional, Personal services, and Entertainment and leisure time. Let's look at them in order.

Professional services

There are no hard rules on who would want to pursue these opportunities. In general, they would appeal to people with business experience. Many will require you have an "office," which could be in your home.

College scholarships and financial guidance. Everyone knows a college education is very expensive, and the costs continue to rise. But financial aid and many little-known scholarships are available. Contact these firms to become an instant expert:

Academic Guidance Services, Inc., 15000R Commerce Pkwy. Mt.Laurel, NJ 08054,

Education Funding and Planning, P.O. Box 771888, Houston, TX 77215,

GO Career Information Center, Inc., P.O. Box 27715, Denver, CO 80227,

Money for College, College Financial Planning Service,, 11846 Balboa Blvd., Granada Hills, CA 91344.

Disability benefits. Many disabled people are not aware of all the Social Security benefits to which they are entitled. You can advise disabled clients on ways to get all of their benefits. Contact Disability Associates, Co., 2615 Harney St., Omaha, NE 68131.

Employment counseling. In this "go-go world" we are seeing more and more changes in companies and in jobs. Both employed and unemployed people would like someone with whom they could discuss and plan their careers. This service could be expanded to include resume preparation and counseling on how to prepare for a job interview.

Income tax preparation and consulting. Each year, millions of people seek help to prepare their tax forms. You have an opportunity to give personalized service and a better price than the big companies in the business. If you are good at this, you can expand to provide tax advice to small businesses. Contact The National Tax Training School, P.O. Box 382, Monsey, NY 10952, or Federated Tax Services, 2021 W. Montrose, Chicago, IL 60618.

Invention broker. Many would-be inventors assume that they have "the better mousetrap" and they soon will be millionaires. Believe me, it is not that simple. You can offer inventors suggestions for improving their invention and provide a business-like approach to contacting companies that might be interested in buying the inventions. Check at your library. There are several good books available on how to go about selling inventions and ideas. Also, see Catalog C15 which discusses inventions. I suggest you work on the basis of a fee plus a percent of the inventor's royalty.

Mortgage reduction expert. You can save your clients thousands of dollars over the term of their home mortgages. Here is a simple example of how you can help them save. Twice a month, pay a little more than half your normal monthly payment. Earlier payments and the small extra amounts will add up to big savings. To learn this approach and help you set up, write to U.S. Mortgage Reduction, P.O. Box 31495, Tucson, AZ 85751, or Mortgage Reduction Consultants, P.O. Box 910, El Dorado, CA 95623.

Property tax reduction expert. You would be amazed at the number of people and companies that are paying too much property tax because of unchallenged property evaluations made by local officials. You can make good money just by being paid a portion of the tax money you save for your clients. Contact American Institute of Property Tax Managers, 615 St.Louis St., Suite 101, Baton Rouge, LA 70802, or Property Tax Publishing Co., Jantzen Office Campus Suite 125, 12200 N. Jantzen Ave., Portland, OR 97217.

Self-improvement counseling and seminars. In this age of "self awareness," there are dozens of opportunities for experienced people to pass on their knowledge to eager clients. Business people want to improve in areas such as appearance and dress, communication skills, and salesmanship. Many of these people would be happy to pay you an excellent hourly fee if you can produce meaningful changes. Conducting group seminars on these same topics can also be both profitable and rewarding. There are companies that will help you to get started with complete programs that are ready to present. For example, contact Carlson Learning Company, Carlson Parkway, P.O. Box 59159, Minneapolis, MN 55459, or Success Motivation Institute, Inc., 5000 Lakewood Dr., Waco, TX 76710.

Caring services

If you are "people-oriented," this category of opportunities gives you a chance to help others. For some, you may be on duty during unusual hours. Also, be sure to check the need for any licenses or special insurance coverage that may be required.

Caring for children.

With more and more parents working, there are a number of necessary services you could provide. Here are a few:

While parents travel. Combining child watching with house sitting could provide good money with very little work. It probably will require night or weekend duty.

After school. Millions of children are being left alone at home after they return from school and before their parents come home from work. You can keep several of these children in your home and offer a number of entertaining and educational activities. Instead of using your home, you might be able to secure a room at a local church for the same activities.

Pickup and delivery. School-age children may be involved in a number of after-school activities which require car rides. You can offer this service, but check local chauffeur license requirements as well as your car insurance coverage.

Summer care and programs. Many school-age children of working parents are on their own during long summer vacations. You can offer a service similar to the "After school" program above. For older children, you can provide a "check-in" service, so that the children have a place to go to spend time, have lunch, and get guidance when they are not out with their friends.

Night and weekend nursery and child care. Most child care centers operate during the normal work week and hours. For the many single parents who must work evenings or weekends, there is a need for child care facilities during their work time.

Caring for the elderly or ill

With more people working, there is a growing problem in our society. More elderly or infirmed people must stay by themselves all day long. Here are some ways you can help:

Home care. Offer a service where you will spend the day with people who need full-time watching.

Daily visits. You can get several "clients" and visit each of them for a short time each day. They would appreciate the visit to relieve monotonous and lonely times. Their families will appreciate the fact that your clients are being checked on every day. You could also include a service to run errands or shop.

Deliver meals. It is difficult for many shut-ins to prepare a meals. You can provide a service to bring warm meals to their homes. You can do this in two ways. You can prepare the meals each day, or you can make arrangements with one or more low-cost restaurants to prepare the meals and you deliver them. The second way has several advantages. You do not have to spend a lot of time in your kitchen. Of equal importance, you can avoid the potential problems of getting local licenses or having inspections by your local heath department.

Courier or transportation services. If you have a car, you can use it to take things to and from shut-ins, whether they are at home or in a hospital. You can also take your clients for rides, to shop, or to various appointments. (Note: as mentioned before, you may need a chauffeur's license as well as adjustments to your car insurance.)

Other caring services

New mothers. The first few weeks home from the hospital after having a baby are difficult times. This is especially true if there are other small children who need care. You can offer a variety of services to the new mother, including shopping, laundering, caring for other children, and meal preparation.

Pets. There are a number of different services you can offer, including sitting while owners are away, daily walks, and grooming. As you get customers, you can offer more than one of these services.

House and apartment sitting. If you are willing to spend nights and weekends in other people's homes, you can perform a number of helpful tasks. There are many people who simply do not like to leave their homes unattended. You can water houseplants and bring in the mail and newspapers to keep a "lived-in" look. While you are there, you can make additional money by taking care of children or pets. You can also provide cleaning and lawn services.

Instructional services

If you have both knowledge and teaching skills, teaching can be a very rewarding experience. People of all ages have either the need or desire to learn, whether it be a language, a musical instrument, a hobby...the list goes on and on. Let's look at a few opportunities:

Tutoring. Many students need help in a particular subject. Tutors provide the individual attention necessary to focus on the student's specific needs in order to learn or master a subject.

Instruction in one topic. It seems that this is an area with endless opportunities. Most of us have something that we do very well. Think about what your expertise is. Would others be interested in learning how you do it? Of equal importance, can you teach the subject well enough so that people would be willing to pay you to learn?

Look at the following typical examples to see if any appeal to you. If not, does the list trigger an idea that you can pursue? (Note: some instruction is best given to one student at a time, while others can be done for groups. What you offer will depend on your subject, the type of students you have, and what they are willing to pay.)

Languages
Ceramics
Dancing
Sewing
Public speaking
Cooking
Carpentry
Sports
Infant care
Art
Musical instruments
Etiquette
Financial planning
Computer usage
Computer programming
Gardening
Car repair
Dog training

One program, which is typical of what you can do, teaches young girls AND boys how to sew using simple patterns and kits. For information, write Kids Can Sew, P.O. Box 1710, St. George, UT 84771.

In addition to the subject, you should also consider:

- The type of student you would like to have (children, elderly, ...)
- When you would like to teach (days, evenings, weekends, ...)
- Where you intend to teach (your home, a school or church, ...)

Personal services

In this category, the emphasis is on offering services of a personal nature.

Basic services. Most of the opportunities listed in this segment will not be new to you. However, they still can yield a good business <u>if you offer something better</u>. Working from your home, you should be able to offer a lower price. You will be avoiding the big expense of renting a business place. If you are willing to work odd hours, you could offer customers the convenience of providing your services in their home at a time convenient for them. In this case, you could charge more, not less. Examples of basic services include:

Hair dressing	Barbering
Manicuring	Hair electrolysis
Tailoring	Laundering and ironing

Roommate matching. In most cities, there are always a number of people looking for roommates to share an apartment—and costs. You will be providing a welcomed service by matching people according to their interests, likes, and dislikes. Develop a simple questionnaire covering your client's interests and the traits they want in a roommate. File these, and develop your own system to retrieve and compare information. (This is a excellent use of a home computer.)

Clothing services. Many business men and women need to keep their appearance neat and in style. They can afford better clothing, but this type of shopping can be very time-consuming. This is were you come in, if you can get several clients. You meet with clients to understand their tastes, and then make specific suggestions on how they can improve their appearance and image. Then, you "shop around" for items you believe they will like and provide a list of recommended items to buy. With some customers, you would actually purchase the clothing, or go with them when they make their purchases.

Private investigator. You may have visions of wild chases with guns drawn and tough talk, but most "P.I." work is business-like and routine. P.I.s are used to investigate insurance claims, locate missing persons, and to perform personal background checks. Before committing to a training program, check with your local police and licensing department to find out what requirements exist in your locality. For information on training courses, write Probe, Inc., P.O. Box 2133, Beverly Hills, CA 90213, or The Rouse School of Special Detective Training, P.O. Box 25750, Santa Ana, CA 92799.

Leisure time and entertainment

Travel. Today, more people have the time, money, and interest to travel. Here are some things you can do to take advantage of this interest.

Cruises. Opening your own travel agency is an expensive proposition. However, there are ways you can get into the cruise part of the travel business without spending a lot of money. Contact The Leisure Group, 58 River St., Milford, CT 06460, or Cruise of a Lifetime, 237 Park Ave., New York, NY 10017.

Bed and breakfast. If you live in an interesting tourist area and can turn a portion of your home over for guests, you can run a successful bed and breakfast business. You have to like people, because you will meet many of them from all walks of life. Write the American Bed and Breakfast Association, Village Green #203, Crofton, MD 21114. A good book is *How to Own and Operate a Bed & Breakfast*, by Jan Stankus, published by Globe Pequot Press, 138 W. Main St., Chester, CT 06412.

Travelogue shows. If you like to travel to exotic and interesting places, you can have your trips make you money. By taking a large number of slides, and maybe some videos, you can come home and put together a show which you can present to civic and church groups and schools. What makes these shows a success is the personal touch you provide with your narrative as well as the ability of the audience to ask questions. If this proves to be a successful business, you can even deduct your trips as business expenses!

Parties

If you have the talent, you can help to make parties a fabulous success. Here are some services you can offer. (If you are a good cook or baker, look at Catalog C2 and C3 for more ideas.)

Party planning. Many career women still want to entertain, but have little time to plan and prepare for a big dinner or party. This is where you come in. You work with the hostess to recommend and plan all phases of the event—flowers, decorations, and the meal. You must know what it takes to orchestrate a successful party. In addition, you should have a list of people you can contact to provide special services, such as food preparation, bar tending, and cleaning before and after.

Provide musicians. If you play a popular instrument, or know people who do, you are off to a good start. Contact several musicians or groups and offer to get them bookings. Then advertise your service.

Piano player. If you have the talent to play different types of popular piano music, you can really liven up a party. Your versatility will help you get more bookings. For example, you can provide soft background music, or honky-tonk rhythm, or music for a sing-along. Piano playing has been successful at holiday parties, children's parties, department store promotions, and style shows, to name a few.

Disk jockey. Even if you cannot play an instrument, you can still provide appropriate music as a hired disk jockey for parties, dances, and special occasions. For information on how to get started, write to the Dallas Agency, P.O. Box 931, Tonawanda, NY 14150.

Bar tender. This does not take as much talent as some of the other opportunities, but you must dress well and know how to make and serve drinks. In today's society, this also means knowing when and how to refuse a drink request from someone who has had enough.

Clowns. Can you imagine having any more fun than you would as a clown? All inhibitions are gone, and the more outlandish your costume, the more people will love you. A clown would be a welcome addition at all but very formal parties. And kids love them! For a good book on clowning, read *Creative Clowning*, by Bruce Fife and others, published by Java Press, 6510 Lehman Dr., Colorado Springs, CO 80918.

Repair services

We have all had times when we did not know where to go to get something fixed. Sometimes when we do find a source, the repair cost is much higher than we expected. If you can supply a needed service at a reasonable price, there are many opportunities in this category. While some require expenses for training, equipment, and parts, others can be started with little money. Here are but a few examples to give you an idea of the range of opportunities:

"Fix-it" shop. If you are one of those fortunate people who can fix just about anything, turn your skills into cash. Among the items you can fix are small appliances, lamps, small furniture pieces, ceramics, knick-knacks, and picture frames, to name a few.

Doll repair. Sometimes these shops are called "doll hospitals" to give them a realistic feeling. Not only do many children love and prize their dolls, but many adults are serious collectors. Repairing different dolls requires a little of many different talents, from sewing, to modeling and painting, to mechanical assembly skills. Keep in mind you must know what you are doing if you agree to work on a valuable doll. For training in doll repair, write to Lifetime Career Schools, 101 Harrison St., Archbald, PA 18403.

Gun repair. This is not one that I would suggest for someone with no previous experience or equipment. However, there are many hunters who repair their own guns. For those with experience and tools, this can be a rewarding business.

VCR repair. Here is an opportunity that has grown rapidly over the past few years. While VCRs are marvels of mechanical and electronic invention, many repairs can be learned by someone with a moderate degree of technical skill. Courses on VCR repair can be purchased from National Electric Controller Co., 4330 Oakton St., Skokie, IL 60076, and Viejo Publications, Inc., 5329 Fountain Ave., Los Angeles, CA 90029.

Bicycle repair. If you have some mechanical skills, there are plenty of sick bicycles that could use your magic. Opportunities range from small children's bikes up to those of the adult enthusiast. To learn all about this business, write to Bicycle Repair of America, Inc., P.O. Box 24106, Minneapolis, MN 55424.

An open mind leaves a chance for someone to drop a worthwhile thought in it - Moses Coit Tyler

C12 Service: for homes and cars

Description: You provide a service (do something) for people's homes or cars.

Concerns: Do you have a way to reach potential customers?

Do you have the expertise to provide the service?

Do you have the necessary equipment?

Check in your community to see if your chosen opportunity has any special requirements for permits or licenses.

Tips: When you work at someone's home, look for ways to advertise your services. Make sure there is a sign on your car or truck. Also, where appropriate, ask homeowners if you can put a sign on their front lawn while you are working at the house. People are funny. If they see work being done on someone else's home, they will become more interested in doing something on theirs.

Don't forget to ask satisfied customers if you can use them as references. Some services have even published a list of references that they distribute with their advertising flyers. But get permission before listing someone!

Examples by type of service

You will be selling a skill for most of these opportunities. Usually you will know if you have the skills because you have been using them in your job or for your own home or car.

I have divided the opportunities into five general categories: Home Improvements, Home Repairs, Cleaning and Maintenance, Car Services, and Other Home Services. Let's look at them in order:

Home improvements

This is an endless opportunity. Millions of homeowners are interested in adding to or improving their homes—if the price is right. If you have the skills, you should be able to compete successfully because of your low overhead costs. Here are a few examples of what you can do:

Home additions and improvements. If you are in this business, you can add extra rooms and storage space in attics or basements. If you have the skills, you can do most of the work yourself. Be aware that even the simplest addition usually requires a multitude of skills and experience, from framing to sheet-rocking, to trimming and painting, and on and on. If you have these skills, great! In addition, you may need help with electrical work, plumbing, and heating and air conditioning. To do this work, you must have a license in most communities. The best way to get this work done is to contract with licensed trades-people.

Home remodeling contractor. This opportunity is similar to the one just described except that you do not have to do any of the construction work. Instead, you meet with homeowners to determine what they want. Then you contract with tradesmen for each job. In this way, you can grow to have several jobs going at one time. For a manual on this opportunity, write MasterCraft Construction, Inc., P.O. Box 30183, Savannah, GA 31410.

Install security systems. People are becoming more concerned about the security of their homes because of the increasing number of reports of burglaries. Recent improvements in technology allow you to install wireless systems thereby avoiding expensive rewiring. You can contact local distributors of these products, or write Alert Companion, 162 - 30 Powells Cove Blvd., Suite 8B, Whitestone, NY 11357.

Build and improve patio decks. People love to be outside in good weather. Many homes would be improved with the addition of a deck for sunning, grilling, and entertaining. A second opportunity is to improve existing patios. They are often unattractive, do not provide any privacy, and may get too hot from the sun. A little creativity and basic carpentry skills can turn these patios into useful and attractive living areas.

Outdoor lighting. This is a growing business. Inexpensive and safe (low voltage) lighting fixtures make it possible to add extra appeal to your home at night while providing additional safety. Lights include spotlights for the house itself, as well as low fixtures along driveways and walkways. Look in your yellow pages for local wholesale suppliers.

Landscaping. An attractive front and back yard can greatly enhance the appearance of any home. What people are looking for is someone who can give advice on what plants to select, where and how to plant them, and how to insure proper drainage. If you can envision how a yard will look and make simple sketches to show your ideas, you can get the business. This could include supplying as well as planting plants. You will need a pickup truck for this one. Also, you will have to establish a working relationship with a nursery to buy plants and trees at wholesale. For a course on landscaping, write Lifetime Career Schools, 101 Harrison Street, Archbald, PA 18403.

Decorate and landscape apartment balconies. Here's one for you city folks. Most apartment dwellers with balconies "decorate" them by putting out two or three inexpensive chairs. Your service can turn even the smallest balcony into another useful living area by introducing design, color, and plants. But watch out. You do not want to make the balcony look unattractive to people passing by outside. Consider that view to provide a "total solution."

Interior decorating. Again, if you have a flair for good design and you have some experience, here is an excellent opportunity. Getting started can be tricky because you might need references as well as good examples of your work for potential clients to see. One good way to get started is to work with a home builder or a furniture store. For a course on interior decorating, contact International Correspondence Schools, 925 Oak St., Scranton, PA 18515.

Paint home numbers on curbs. Here is a good example of how a simple idea can bring in extra money. It is a great idea for high school or college students because it requires salesmanship, perseverance, and just the smallest amount of talent. Going door to door, you offer to paint the home number on the curb in front of the house, where it can readily be seen. Using a stencil, you spray paint a black box about 5 inches high by 12 inches long. Now, using stencils of the house numbers, spray paint the numbers in white paint. If you charge $3 to $5, you can easily make $50 to $150 over a weekend. Not bad! You can buy stencils from artist supply stores, or you can buy a complete starter kit from Magic Systems, P.O. Box 23888, Tampa, FL 33623.

Organize closet space. There never seems to be enough storage space. Experts in closet organization can often double the amount of space available. They do it by rethinking what a closet should look like, while taking advantage of new products designed to improve closet efficiency.

Winterize and watch over summer homes. If you live near a resort area where there are many summer homes, you can provide a number of services for the home owners. For example, you can winterize and close up the home after the summer season. You can visit the homes every few weeks throughout the off-season to make sure there are no problems. If an owner would like to make a winter visit, you can open the home and provide a cleaning service. If you can get a number of clients, you will be making money with very little effort.

Install custom-made awnings. Attractive home awnings provide protection from the sun while enhancing the appearance of a home. They come in a wide variety of designs, from small, permanent window models to 40-foot long models that open and close automatically by sensing the sun. You work with homeowners to design an awning to meet their needs. Fabrics come in a wide variety of colors and designs. The manufacturer then provides you with the awning ready to install. For more information, contact Anchor Industries, Inc., 1100 Burch Drive, P.O. Box 3477, Evansville, IN 47733.

Home repairs

The fix-it business will always be needed. With more working people and single parent families, people do not have either the time or skill to do everything. Here are some opportunities you should consider:

Handyman (or handywoman) service. Are you one of those people who can tackle just about any repair job around your home? Why not offer these same talents to the many people who do not have them? Here is a hint. Advertise that "no job is too small." You will get all the business you can handle, and many of them will be big jobs. Many companies ignore small jobs because they cannot charge enough. This can be just the opportunity for you to get started. Warning: Do not tackle those jobs that require a licensed tradesman, such as electrical or plumbing work. There are plenty of other tasks that do not require a trade license. Stick to those and stay away from potential problems.

Specific repair services. Many people are making a comfortable living by specializing in one type of home repair. Working from their homes, and often on their own, they can offer a price advantage to their customers. At the same time, if they do quality work, they can control that quality by staying small and not hiring help with unknown abilities. Some examples include:

Wallpapering
House painting
Tile and grout repair
Bathtub and sink repair and refinishing
Kitchen cabinet door replacing
Kitchen counter repair and refinishing
Tightening creaking floors

Reupholster and repair furniture. Most people do not have direct experience in this field. However, many have the basic skills and experience necessary to learn the business quickly. For information, write Foley-Belsaw Institute of Upholstery, 6301 Equitable Rd., Box 593, Kansas City, MO 64141.

Vinyl repair. There are many items in the average household that are made of vinyl plastic. One of the most common is leather-like chair coverings, which are subject to tears and burns. There are now kits available that will allow you to accurately match the color and texture of most vinyl materials. Incidentally, this opportunity is even larger when you consider car seats and tops, as well as the number of businesses that use vinyl furniture. You can contact:

Repair-It Industries, Inc., 440 W. Hopocan Ave., Barberton, OH 44203,

Fitzgerald's, 2221 E. Minor Ave., Stockton, CA 95205,

Vinyl Industrial Products, 2021 W. Montrose Ave., Chicago, IL 60618.

Repair countertops. Over time, many kitchen and bathroom countertops get scratched, discolored, or burnt, and replacing them can be expensive. You can provide a service to make them like new and save the homeowner a great deal of money. For a course and materials, contact Renew-All, 516 SE Chkalov Drive, Suite 202, Vancouver, WA 98684.

Small engine repair. Think of all the small devices used in yards that are powered by small gas engines. These include lawn mowers, chain saws, clippers, and snow blowers. These millions and millions of devices need service sooner or later. Why shouldn't you provide that service? You can learn all about this opportunity, including how to make repairs by contacting Foley-Belsaw Institute of Small Engine Repair, 6301 Equitable Rd., Box 593, Kansas City, MO 64141.

Other things that need fixing. While it is easy to find a repair service for some items, others are far more difficult to find. Consider:

Furniture repair and refinishing
Antiques repair
Old clock repair
A "fix-it" shop, for repairs of all kinds of things

Cleaning and maintenance

Many of these services have the advantage of repeat business. Once you get a customer base, you can have a fairly steady income. Also, several opportunities can be combined to allow you to make more money. Let's look at a list of examples that do not require much money to get started:

House cleaning
Lawn and yard care
Indoor plant care
Swimming pool maintenance
Power-wash cleaning of home exteriors, driveways, and sidewalks
Attic, basement, and garage clean-out
Window and screen cleaning
Rain gutter clean-out
Chimney cleaning
Venetian blind repair and cleaning

For a course on how to set up a cleaning service, contact Professional Cleaning Associates, P.O. Box 734, Hurst, TX 76053, or Cleaning Consultant Services, 1512 Western Ave., P.O. Box 1273, Seattle, WA 98111. A good book on the subject is *Cleaning up For a Living*, by Don Aslett and Mark Browning, published by Betterway Publications, P.O. Box 219, Crozet, VA 22932.

Car services

While there are many businesses catering to the needs of car owners, there are still opportunities available for the small business person. As with other opportunities, you have to look for what is missing or should be improved and provide that service. Here are some examples:

Mobile car repairs, tune-ups, oil changes. For the convenience of your customers, you go to their cars! Car repairs are a downright inconvenience for many people. They would be happy if you would go to their homes to make simple repairs and tune-ups in their driveways or garages. There is a catch to this. The necessary tools and equipment can be expensive. Unless you already have them or can get a good deal, you might not meet this book's objectives of low startup costs. To start, you can limit your expenses in two ways. You can limit the kinds of repairs you can make or you can limit repairs to one or two makes of cars.

Car repair estimates. To start, you must be an experienced mechanic. Your service is to provide an independent estimate of what it should cost to repair a car. You do not make the repairs yourself, which will give your clients confidence in the honesty of your estimate. You charge a fee based on the time it will take you to develop the estimate. You can offer this service to two groups of people; those facing expensive repairs on their cars, and those who are considering buying a used car.

Windshield repairs. It is very easy for a windshield to be damaged or scratched. This minor damage can be annoying, yet most of the cost to replace the windshield could fall within the deductible amount of your car insurance. Several companies offer products to make inexpensive repairs without replacing the windshield. Write to:

Glass Mechanix, Inc., 10170 N.W. 47th St., Sunrise, FL 33351,

Glas-Weld Systems, 63065 Sherman Rd., Bend, OR 97701,

Grubb's Glass Patch, P.O. Box 243, Monticello, AR 71655.

Car polishing. This is another business you can operate by going to the customer's home or business to work on the car. To get the best results (and charge accordingly) you need good equipment. You can check at local auto supply companies, or write to Polishing Systems, P.O. Box 1512, New Castle, PA 16103, or Cyclo Manufacturing Company, 1438 S. Cherokee St., P.O. Box 2038, Denver, CO 80201.

Other home services

Garage sales. People shy away from having a garage sale because it takes too much planning and time. If you offer to run the entire sale for a percent of the money received, you should get plenty of interest. Running a successful sale requires advertising, pricing, displaying merchandise, and record keeping. If you would like to become an "instant authority," get a copy of the manual *Garage Sale Mania*, by Chris Stevenson, published by Betterway Publications, P.O. Box 219, Crozet, VA 22932.

Recycling. In a few communities, this is no longer an opportunity, since they are providing a system for the recycling of newspapers, glass, plastics, and aluminum. However, there is still plenty of opportunity in most cities and towns. Probably the easiest way to start would be to collect old newspapers, which you can then sell to paper processors. Since you will not get paid much per pound, you will need a pickup truck to collect enough volume to pay off. If you would like to try a more exotic recycling opportunity, consider gold and silver. For a manual, write L.C. Meredith, P.O. Box 11216, Reno, NV 89510.

Accident-proof homes. A majority of accidents still take place in the home. Many involve children. Quite often these accidents could have been avoided by making simple changes or educating parents. For example, handles of hot pots should always be turned away from the front of the stove so that they cannot be accidentally struck by children. There are many new inexpensive devices available today to keep young children out of cabinets, drawers, and electric sockets. Take some time to read up on the subject. Many insurance companies have free booklets on home safety. Then talk to various parents groups and day care centers to generate interest in your service.

Document possessions. Here is a service that most people would prefer not to need, but it would be extremely valuable in critical times. For a fee, you go through a home and make a list of all valuable possessions. Photos should be taken of important items. The final package is kept in a secure place. In case of fire or a burglary, the list would help to settle insurance claims. For information, contact Property Documentation Services, 2116 E. Arapaho, #111, Richardson, TX 75081.

Inspect homes. This one is not for beginners. But if you have experience and knowledge in building trades, this is a great opportunity. More and more people are seeking independent evaluations of homes before buying. The amount they pay for this service is much less than the hassle involved to correct faulty construction. To provide the proper service, you should be knowledgeable in all phases of construction and know local building codes.

Locksmithing. People are forever losing keys, breaking locks, or wanting them changed. If you have mechanical skills you can learn this business quickly. For a complete course of instruction with startup materials, contact Foley-Belsaw Institute of Locksmithing, 6301 Equitable Rd., P.O. Box 593, Kansas City, MO 64141, or Locksmithing Institute, 1500 Cardinal Drive, Little Falls, NJ 07424.

"Impossible" is a word I never say - Collin d'Harville

C13 Service: for businesses

Description: You provide a service (do something) for other businesses.

Concerns: Do you have a way to reach potential customers?

Do you have the expertise to provide the service?

Do you have the necessary equipment?

Is the economy healthy so that business owners will have money for your services?

Is your service seasonal in nature so that you will make most of your money during a relatively short period?
If so, will you have enough money to carry you the rest of the year?

Tips: Selling to businesses is different from selling to individuals. More businesses will want you to extend credit to delay paying you. Be prepared by knowing what your standard payment terms will be. You should also be prepared to make some adjustments to your terms rather than lose an important sale.

Examples by type of service

The categories used in this segment are: Consulting services, Sales assistance, Maintenance and repair, and Other services for businesses.

Consulting services

If you have some business experience and can project a professional image, there are a number of opportunities that you can consider.

Business consultant. Do you have experience and expertise acquired during your own work experience? Perhaps other businesses can use your knowledge. More business people are choosing this approach because it provides challenge and independence. It can also be very lucrative. You will need a proven track record plus the ability to sell yourself and your capabilities. For a detailed manual on this subject, get a copy of *The Consultant's Kit: Establishing and Operating Your Own Consulting Business*, from Dr. Jeffrey Lant. Write Dr. Jeffrey Lant, 50 Follen Street, Cambridge, MA 02138.

Conduct training seminars and programs. In this world of constant change, the need for employee training programs continues to grow. Most businesses cannot afford the expense of creating and running their own programs. This is where you come in. There are a number of companies offering excellent ready-to-go programs covering subjects such as teamwork, planning, quality control, customer satisfaction, and so on. There are also numerous programs on self-improvement, communication skills, and salesmanship. If you can speak well and have a professional appearance, this can be a rewarding opportunity. For more information, contact:

Carlson Learning Company, Carlson Parkway, P.O. Box 59159, Minneapolis, MN 55459,

Success Motivation Institute, 5000 Lakewood Dr., Waco, TX 76710.

In addition, here is a company that can provide you with a number of sources for these programs. Dynamic Development Associates, P.O. Box 18, Media, PA 19063.

If you have expertise in a subject and would like to develop and conduct your own workshop, there is a great deal of information you will need to be successful. An excellent manual you should read is *Money Talks: The Complete Guide to a Profitable Workshop or Seminar in Any Field*, by Dr. Jeffrey Lant. Write Dr. Jeffrey Lant, 50 Folley St., Suite 507, Cambridge, MA 02138.

Public speaking. Speaking at professional, educational, and business conferences, conventions, and other functions can be very profitable. Although there are exceptions, you should meet two basic requirements to command a reasonable fee. You should be a good speaker AND you should be an authority on the subject you are talking about. You will find that most public speakers have a basic business built around their expertise. They use speaking to generate additional income and new business for their basic business by speaking to potential clients. Used in this way, public speaking is a natural tie-in with the consulting and seminar opportunities described earlier.

For more information on public speaking, consider subscribing to *Sharing Ideas Among Professional Speakers*, an excellent newsletter published by the well-known speaker Dottie Walters, 2014 Siegle Drive, Lemon Grove, CA 92045.

Also, write to Speakers USA, Inc., P.O. Box 1460, Pigeon Forge, TN 37868. If you join this association, you will be entitled to attend excellent free seminars covering various aspects of the speaking business.

Business loan consultant. There are always small businesses that need more money to continue to operate or grow. There are a number of reasons why loans may be difficult to obtain. One of the biggest is not knowing how or where to get help. If you have experience in this area you should have little trouble finding clients. Your list of sources for potential loans should include banks, private investors, and the Small Business Administration. Knowing what the different types of lenders need to know to make a decision and providing that information in a business-like fashion will significantly improve your chances for success.

Mortgage loan broker. This is similar to the business loan consultant, but here you specialize in providing sources of mortgage money for commercial builders and developers. Typical projects include office buildings, apartment complexes, and shopping centers. You charge a small fee, but since you are working on large loans, you can earn a substantial commission. Write to American Fidelity Mortgage Corp., 8033 Eberly Ave., North Charleston, SC 29420.

Business broker. For a number of reasons there are always people eager to sell their businesses. At the same time, other people are just as eager to buy. A business broker acts to bring these people together to see if a mutually beneficial sales agreement can be reached. One easy way to get started is to sell advertisements for a publication that tries to bring buyers and sellers together. If this is of interest to you, contact Associates Assistance Company, 4507 W. 8th St., Drawer 58201, Cincinnati, OH 45258.

Small computer expert. If you are an expert on small computers, this is a great opportunity. As the price of computers comes down, more businesses need and want them. But many small business owners do not know which computer or programs to buy, how to set up the system, or how to use it. This problem can cost them a great deal of time and money. In addition, if they buy from a computer dealer, they may end up with a system that the dealer has in stock, rather than the best one for the job. Because you are independent, you can advertise that you will make the best recommendations based on the owners needs and budget. Among the services you can provide are:

Computer and other equipment selection
Application software selection
Customizing software to meet business needs
Design and selection of forms
Layout and furniture selection
Installation and checkout
Operator and user education

For a good book, look for *How to Make Money with Your Desktop Computer*, by Herman Holtz, Published by John Wiley & Sons, New York.

Conduct market research and surveys. If you have some experience in this area, there are <u>many</u> small businesses that could use your help. As competition for the dollar increases, businesses need to know more about their customers and what they want. A good questionnaire properly administered can provide company owners with invaluable information to improve their competitiveness and customer service.

Teach in stores. Are you good at some do-it-yourself activity? Why not contact a local lumber yard and offer to conduct evening classes on such topics as basic carpentry, or deck building, or plumbing? Why not set up a sewing class in a fabric shop, or teach simple car repairs at a local garage or auto supply shop? People are eager to learn and save money, and businesses that offer to help will gain loyal customers.

Property tax reduction. Many businesses are paying too much tax because tax appraisers have appraised their property too high. Your service can save some businesses thousands of dollars every year. Incidentally, this same business can be applied to homes. To learn more about this opportunity, contact American Institute of Property Tax Managers, 615 St. Louis St., Suite 101, Baton Rouge, LA 70802.

Theft protection. Retailers lose millions of dollars every year from shoplifting and employee theft. There are many things that store owners can do to reduce their losses. Without previous experience, you can sell and conduct educational programs on theft reduction as long as you have the right teaching materials. One source that can provide everything you would need is the Small Business Advancement Institute, Crime Prevention Unit, 33 N. Central Ave., Suite 213, Medford, OR 97501.

Testing service for prospective employees. Let's face it. The caliber of the people hired by a company can significantly affect the company's efficiency and profit. You can provide a service that helps company owners select the right people by providing an evaluation of people applying for work. For information, contact Gold Coast Professional Solutions, Inc., 2245 First St., Suite 104, Simi Valley, CA 93065.

Be a publicist. Here is a business you can quickly develop if you are good with people, have an active imagination, and can write well. Most business people would love to have complimentary articles in their local newspapers about themselves or their companies. It is good for their egos—and good for business. Talk to your clients to find interesting things about them. This could be a wide variety of topics, from growth of the company to a recent interesting trip to something outstanding about a family member. You write the story and submit it to the local newspaper. Good, clear photographs will help. To learn more, one book to look for is *Publicity: How to*, by Martin Pollack, Published by Alliance Pubs., P.O. Box 25004, Ft. Lauderdale, FL 33320.

Sales assistance

Companies large and small are always looking for ways to improve sales. Here are some businesses that might help them.

Telephone sales. Do you enjoy talking on the phone? Or are you forced to stay at home because of a handicap or family situation? Here is an interesting way to make money. Contract with local small businesses to make telephone calls to potential customers advising them of a special sale or promotion. You tell the business owner that you do not expect a set fee or salary, but want a commission on all business you generate. This plan can work in several ways. If the small business is a retail store with a customer list, you can use that list for your calls. If the small business requires you to get new customers, such as house painters or home improvement specialists, you will have to make "cold calls." Names and phone numbers in a neighborhood can be easily found at your public library. The following references list telephone numbers and homeowners' names by street: *Cross Reference Directory*, published by City Publishing Company, Independence, KS., and *Polk City Directory*, published by R.L. Polk Co., Richmond, VA.

Prepare and distribute advertising flyers. One of the most effective ways to advertise is through one-sheet flyers that are delivered door to door. Many small business owners are unaware of this. Others do it themselves in such an amateurish way that it fails to get results. If you are good with words and have some artistic talents you can quickly get into business. If you have access to a personal computer and laser printer, all the better. Sell a full service. Design the flyer, contract with a local print shop to produce the flyers, then arrange to have local teenagers distribute them.

Create new ways to advertise. If you are creative, put your imagination to work to create new inexpensive ways to advertise. Small businesses need to advertise, but often cannot afford the traditional ways. Some creative people have sold advertising space on park benches and on bulletin boards placed in airports, hotel lobbies, and retail stores. Others have sold streamers attached to pizza delivery cars. Still others have negotiated with restaurants to provide free menus on which they have sold advertisements to nearby businesses. Most schools need scoreboards for sports events but have no money to pay for anything but a basic unit. Some schools are now getting free scoreboards by allowing local businesses to place paid advertisements on them.

Conduct seminars on customer service. More than ever before, customer service is recognized as a critical factor for a company to succeed. There is a need to train sales personnel, medical personnel, and others who come in contact with customers and patients. One company that specializes in developing this type of program is Service Quality Institute, 9201 E. Bloomington Frwy., Minneapolis, MN 55420.

Maintenance and repair

Consider offering services that do not require a great deal of training. Here are several examples:

Flat roof repairs. It is common knowledge that flat roofs can develop leaks, and permanent repairs can be expensive. Many business buildings have this type of roof. If you are interested in selling products that can be easily applied by your business customer's maintenance man (you do not have to apply it), contact Pace Products, Inc., Quality Plaza, 11775 W. 112th St., P.O. Box 10925, Overland Park, KS 66210.

Refill laser printer and copier cartridges. Talk about growth! The number of office devices that use toner cartridges has grown into the millions in a few short years. Until recently, users had to buy new cartridges whenever the toner was depleted. Now several companies offer training and equipment so that the old cartridges can be reused by cleaning them and refilling them with additional toner. If you are interested in providing this service, write to Laser Product Consultants, 18804 N. Creek Pkwy., Suite 115, Bothell, WA 98011.

Office and store cleaning service. If you can get just a few businesses to buy your cleaning service you can do quite well financially. All you need is a few cleaning aids and supplies. Concentrate on small businesses because the larger ones either have their own people or use large cleaning services. Any company that hires you will want you to be reliable, neat, and thorough while not disrupting normal work procedures. Many will not want you on their premises after work hours. For manuals on cleaning businesses, write Cleaning Consultant Services, Inc., 1512 Western Ave., P.O. Box 1273, Seattle, WA 98111.

Another opportunity for cleaning is in newly-built homes or vacated homes and apartments. Your service might clean empty homes and apartments to make them easier to sell or lease. Contact builders and real estate agents to offer this service.

Invisible weaving. Here is a technique that will allow you to reweave damaged fabric to be good as new. Tears, burns, and moth holes seem to disappear. You can offer this service to friends. Better, go to local dry cleaners, formal-wear rental shops, and clothing stores and tell them about your services. For information on a course, write Fabricon Company, 2021 W. Montrose, Chicago, IL 60618.

Other repair opportunities for businesses. A number of the opportunities described in Catalog C12, under "Home improvements" and "Home repairs" can be used for businesses as well. If you have not done so, I recommend you spend time reviewing C12 to determine if there are opportunities that you would like to apply to businesses. A few examples that come to mind are:

Install security systems
Interior decorating
Handyman services
Small remodeling jobs
Vinyl furniture repair
Awning design and installations

Other services for businesses

There are many other opportunities for business services that do not fit the categories we just reviewed. Here are some examples.

Install draperies and blinds. Many companies and interior decorators that sell window drapes and blinds would rather concentrate on the design and selling aspect of the business and not install the products themselves. This is where you come in if you are a careful person and know how to use a few basic tools. You can contract with several of these companies or decorators to do the installation. For more information, contact Mountain Draperies, P.O. Box 27655, Lakewood, CO 80227.

Telephone answering service. There is no question that telephone answering machines are being used by an increasing number of businesses. However, there is also a growing dissatisfaction by customers with the impersonal nature and inconvenience associated with these gadgets. Operating from your home, you can offer an answering service for the many businesses that want to keep a "personal touch" with their customers. Modern telephone equipment and switching techniques make this an easy business to get started. Contact your local telephone business office for information on available services.

Decorate store windows. Did you ever notice that some store windows are very attractive and well decorated while others are drab and not very appealing? If you have an artistic flair, why not offer your services to design and decorate those drab windows? Once you have the interest of store owners, spend some time talking to them to understand their business. Then make up some sketches to illustrate several proposed designs. Once you have the owner's approval, you can implement the selected design. One of the nice things about this business is that you do not spend money until <u>after</u> you get the order to proceed.

The important thing is not to stop questioning - Albert Einstein

C14 Creative: for resale

Description: You produce items and sell them, directly or indirectly, to customers. These are often "one-of-a-kind" originals or items with just a few copies.

Concerns: Do you have the expertise to make salable items?

Can you make enough money to satisfy your needs? Many people use these businesses to keep busy and supplement other income, not as their sole source of income.

Do you have a way to reach potential customers?

Can you travel to attend shows outside your area? This could increase your opportunity for sales, but travel takes time and money.

Is there a demand for your products?

Will enough people want your products?

How will your products fare against competition?

Do you have enough money, equipment, and supplies to create the inventory you will need?

Is your business seasonal in nature so that you will make most of your money during a relatively short time? If so, will you have enough money to carry you for the rest of the year?

Tips: If you do not know how to start, I strongly recommend you attend local craft fairs and flea markets and get to know some of the regular sellers. Ask questions. You will find that there is excellent comradeship among these people. You can also read the books listed under "Getting started," page 240.

Marketing: Usually the biggest problem is to sell sufficient quantities of your items to make the money you need. There are a number of ways that have been used, including:

Flea markets and craft fairs.

Stands in shopping malls.

Selling to stores for resale.

Placing items on consignment in retail stores.

Mail order.

Setting up a selling area in an extra room in your home or in your garage.

Forming a cooperative with other crafts people and, as a group, renting space to show your wares.

Pricing: Deciding how to price your work is a frequent problem. As a newcomer, your first step is to determine what other people are charging for comparable work. You can either charge more or less, depending on your honest appraisal of how the quality and attractiveness of your work compares with the competition. After you have been in business a while, you will develop a sense for how to price. If you are really talented and can make items with high demand, you can charge "what the market will bear." That is why one artist gets $25 for a painting and another artist gets $50,000. For more on pricing, see Lesson 31.

Examples:

Art and Crafts. This is a very broad and diverse field. Most readers are aware of the more popular items, such as:

Painting
Sculpture
Ceramics
Pottery

Photography
Jewelry
Sewn items
Knit items
Wood crafts
Leather products
Stained glass items
Rock polishing

Here are just a few other items that people have turned into money:

Driftwood sculpture
Totem poles
Bird carvings
Flower baskets
Christmas ornaments
Tie-dyed T-shirts
Pine cone decorations
Decorative plates
Wall plaques
Mobiles
Dried flower arrangements
Candle making

Make-to-order custom crafts (also, see Catalog C3)

Drawing caricatures
Calligraphy
Custom lamp shades
Personalized wood desk signs and wall plaques
Paintings of:
- Family members
- Residences
- Pets
- Store fronts

Other creative opportunities

Repairing and refurbishing antiques and "junque."
Making lamps and knickknacks from old car parts.
Creating and producing marionette or puppet shows.
If you are a traveler, creating travel slide shows.

Getting started

I can assume that if you are interested in starting a craft business you are experienced and good at your chosen craft. Perhaps you learned the craft as a hobby. However, you may need help with the business and marketing aspects. Here are two excellent books: *Crafts Marketing Success Secrets*, by Barbara Brabec, published by Brabec Productions, P.O. Box 2137, Naperville, IL 60567, and *How to Sell What You Make*, by Paul Gerhards, published by Stackpole Books, P.O. Box 1831, Cameron and Keller Sts., Harrisburg, PA 17105.

If you are interested in art as a career, here are two good books: *This Business of Art,* by Diane Cochrane, published by Ayer Co. Pubs, Inc., P.O. Box 958, Salem, NH 03079, and *Living By Your Brush Alone*, by Edna Piersol, published by North Lights Books, 1507 Dana Ave., Cincinatti, OH 454207.

With your experience, you probably have some equipment and know where to get the materials you need. If you cannot buy supplies locally, a guide which describes more than 2600 sources throughout the country is *The Crafts Supply Sourcebook: A Comprehensive Shop-by-Mail Guide*, by Margaret Boyd, published by Betterway Publications, P.O. Box 219, Crozet, VA 22932. Here are a few examples of what you can buy:

Lynnette Company, Inc. — Cast plaster molds
6251 Mentor Park Blvd., Mentor, OH 44060

Pinecraft Woodworks — Plans for quality wooden toy trucks
Rt. 4, P.O. Box 4071, Burley, ID 83318

Pourette Mfg. Co. — Candle making equipment and molds
6910 Roosevelt Way N.E., P.O. Box 15220, Seattle, WA 98115

Enterprise Art — Jewelry, doll, and craft supplies
P.O. Box 2918, Largo, FL 34649

Cherry Tree Toys, Inc. — Plans and parts for wood projects
P.O. Box 369, Belmont, OH 43718

Castings — Molds for cast lead soldiers
P.O. Box 915001, Longwood, FL 32791

Your imagination, my dear fellow, is worth more than you imagine -
Louis Aragon

C15 Creative: for production

Description: You develop an item and sell the "master" to a company that mass produces and distributes it. You could get paid a fixed amount or a royalty. Activities I discuss include writing, commercial art, song writing, and inventing.

Concerns: While there is the possibility of making big money, many of these endeavors are tough to crack. Be prepared for rejection and long periods of negotiation.

Do you have the expertise to develop a salable item?

Are you realistic in assessing the value of your idea?

Do you have a way to reach companies that might buy your idea?

Do you have the skill and experience to sell your idea to company executives?

Can you show there will be a demand for your product ideas?

Can you wait a relatively long time for a company to make a decision to accept your proposal?

Tips: <u>Do your homework</u>.

For most creative people, the biggest problem is putting a practical value on their ideas. Try to be honest with yourself. I have talked with dozens of authors, artists, and inventors who are convinced that they have a project that will make them instant millionaires. Yes, this can happen, but it rarely does.

Creative people tend to think that the worth of their ideas will be obvious to anyone who looks at the project. However, companies will perform a careful analysis of any project before committing to produce it. You can improve your chances by presenting your project in a business-like manner and by providing whatever information you can to show that your project would bring profit to the company.

Selling your ideas through agents

Trying to reach companies that would like to take over and produce your ideas can be very difficult and frustrating. You might choose to work through an agent or representative to reach these companies.

WARNING: While there are many legitimate and conscientious agents and reps, there are many who are not. The legitimate ones will accept you as a client only after they judge that you have a good idea that has a reasonable chance of being bought by a company. In a few instances, they may require a small amount of "up-front" money from you, but they will make most of their money by taking a share (commission or fee) from any money they negotiate for you. If they ask for money, understand the reason why.

The questionable agents will tell you that your idea is great, but they will need money from you so that they can study and analyze the idea further. In this way, they make money from you whether or not your idea is sold (and it rarely is).

Here are some precautions you can take to help you select an agent:

- Talk with more than one agent and go with the one who best suits your needs.
- Beware of lavish praise of your ideas and promises of big money.
- Ask to see examples of what the agent has done for other clients and understand how the agent plans to go about representing you.
- Ask for client references. If possible, talk to the clients to see how satisfied they are with the agent.
- If you have any doubts, do not sign an agreement with an agent.

This is especially important if you have to pay money at the time of the signing.

- See your lawyer <u>before</u> you sign anything.

- If the agent turns <u>you</u> down, understand why. Is it because he or she is very successful and too busy to take on more clients, or is it because there is lack of confidence in your idea?

Examples:

Writing

You can use your writing skills in a number of ways. If writing is your area of interest, you <u>must</u> become familiar with several books that can provide invaluable information, guidance, and the names of hundreds of important industry contacts. These books include *Writer's Market*, *Novel and Story Writer's Market*, and *Poet's Market*, produced annually by Writer's Digest Books, and published by F & W Publishers, 1507 Dana Ave., Cincinatti, OH 45207. You should find one or more of these books at your local library.

Books. An amazing number of people harbor a hidden desire to write a book. Here are some examples of book-length writing opportunities:

Novels
Non-fiction: history, technical, travel, how-to, etc.
Children's books
Cookbooks
Poetry

Getting a book published can be a very frustrating experience. While there are over 6,000 publishers in the United States, competition is fierce. About 10% of all book ideas submitted to publishers actually get published. In addition, publication does not guarantee that the author will make much money. While a few authors command huge advance payments and are millionaires, most authors can expect modest financial gain for their efforts.

If you are serious about book writing, you should be aware that you do not have to write the complete book before contacting a publisher. The editors who decide which books a publisher will accept are busy people. They do not have the time to read complete books to make their decisions. Instead, you should submit a book proposal which you must count on to sell yourself—your knowledge, ideas, and writing skills.

Your proposal must be complete, neat, and professional. It should include:

1. Title of the proposed book.

2. Table of Contents.

3. A brief marketing story, covering why you believe your book is marketable. Use what you learned in Lesson 19, Exercise 6. Who would buy your book? How many of these people are there? Why would they buy your book? What does your book have over the competition (similar books currently being sold)?

4. Your credentials. What makes you an expert on the topic?

5. **For non-fiction:** A detailed outline of each chapter. You should include samples of pictures, illustrations, or charts, if you intend to use them.

   For fiction: A story outline which illustrates the setting, main characters, and plot. In addition, you will need to provide drafts of your first few chapters which reflect your writing style and plot development.

For more information on how to get your work in print, an excellent, easy-to-read book is *How to Get Happily Published*, by Judith Applebaum, published by Harper & Row, 10 E. 53rd St. New York, NY 10022. If you are interested in self-publishing, see Catalog C4.

Magazine articles. There has been an explosion of new magazines, giving writers new opportunities to get their articles published. You might assume that the number of magazines seen on a newsstand is representative of all that are published. Not so. There are thousands of trade and regional magazines that most of us will never see. To get a full listing, check your library for copies of *Gale Directory of Publication & Broadcast Media*, published by Gale Research, or *The Standard Periodical Directory*, published by Oxbridge Communications, Inc.

The Writer's Digest books mentioned earlier give detailed listings on many magazines looking for articles. Select magazines that best match your favorite topics. A word of warning—it is difficult for a newcomer to have an article accepted by the big-name magazines. Start with smaller magazines, but remember that they usually do not pay much. That's okay. You need to build a proven track record first.

Writing for companies. While all companies need well-written manuals, reports, and brochures, many cannot afford to hire all the writers they could use. Therefore, they will contract for outside help. In addition, greeting-card manufacturers need help for writing verses. The books published by Writer's Digest, mentioned earlier, list hundreds of firms with writing opportunities.

Writing for newspapers. If you are an expert in a topic with a great deal of reader interest, such as gardening, car or home repairs, even food shopping, you may be able to start a column in a local paper. Prepare two or three good sample columns and visit the paper's editor. You will not make much money writing for just one small paper, but if readers like your column, you can contact other out-of-town papers and offer them the same service. And if you are really good, you can expand your "syndication," and appear in many newspapers throughout the country. That's when the money can really multiply! For more information, look for the book *How to Write and Sell a Column*, by Julie Raskin and Carolyn Males, produced by Writer's Digest.

Here is another idea. Did you ever notice the tiny articles inserted in newspapers that really are not news but are of general interest to readers? They are called "fillers" and are used by the people who arrange newspaper pages to fill blank spaces between articles. You cannot get rich, but you can have fun writing these for local newspapers. Contact editors to see if there is a need for fillers. It would be a good idea to do some research and create a few samples to take with you. Make sure the fillers are short, well-written, and interesting. As with newspaper columns, once you get started, you may be able to sell your service to other newspapers.

Commercial Art: Art for business

As with writers, businesses have many needs for good artists, designers, and photographers. Since workload will vary throughout the year, there are many opportunities for freelancers. In general, commercial art is drawn to order as specified by the requesting company. The first thing you should do is get a copy of *Artist's Market*, produced annually by Writer's Digest, published by F & W Publishers, 1507 Dana Ave., Cincinatti, OH 45207. Like the writer's books, it provides excellent information and guidance, plus hundreds of contacts to sell just about any kind of art.

Art and photographs for reproductions, calendars, posters, and greeting cards. These are areas where original ideas and designs are accepted. For a comprehensive list of companies that are looking for help, see *Artist's Market*.

Advertising and brochure art. These assignments tend to be more specific. If you are good, clients will tend to keep you because your art style could provide consistency throughout an advertising campaign. Clients could include businesses, advertising agencies, audio/visual studios, art studios, and book publishers. Again, see *Artist's Market*.

Writing popular music

The popular music business is very competitive—and complicated. It is not easy for a new songwriter to break into it. Knowing about the business will improve your chances of success and reduce the possibility of making a serious mistake. For a detailed description of the business, you must get a copy of *Song Writer's Market*, produced annually by Writer's Digest, published by F & W Publications, Cincinatti, OH 45207. It is an excellent reference with practical information and advice on all aspects of the music business. What to do, where to go, and who to contact are all covered in detail. Your local library should have it.

Assuming you have songs you would like to sell, here is a brief summary of the steps you should take:

- You need a demonstration (demo) cassette recording of your song or songs. Make sure it is a good quality recording so that the music and lyrics are clearly presented. Of course, you want to make the best impression possible, but be careful. You could spend a small fortune hiring professional musicians and a sound studio and equipment.

- Spend time reviewing books such as *Song Writer's Market* to learn which companies in the music industry you should contact with your type of song. The book also details each company's requirements for how to submit songs.

- Follow the requirements and send a cassette with a copy of your lyrics to the appropriate contacts.

- To protect your songs from being stolen (not a problem with the reputable companies), you should keep good records. Keep records, with dates, showing each revision. Copyrighting your songs is the best protection. See *Song Writer's Market* for what to do.

Writing computer programs

The microcomputer (personal computer) industry has experienced phenomenal growth. In a dozen years, microcomputers have grown from being a curious and expensive toy to becoming a necessity for millions of businesses and families. The original computers were difficult to use and required an in-depth knowledge of how they worked. As public demand grew, manufacturers quickly realized that "ease-of-use" was an important selling feature. The new users were only interested in what the computer could do for them, not how the computer did it. They wanted instant solutions to fix a problem or to help them with their work. They did not want to spend long hours learning how to write programs to get their work done.

Application programs. Application programs, along with improvements to the computers, are the answers. These programs are written to perform a specific task, or series of tasks, such as word processing, spread sheets, and bookkeeping, to name just a few of the bigger programs. There are thousands of smaller programs that perform smaller, more specific tasks, such as home budgets, income tax preparation, teaching aids, and games.

If you can write programs, there is still plenty of opportunity available to make money. To improve your chances, you should consider the following factors:

The program

- What system(s) will it work on?
- What are the memory requirements?
- Is it easy-to-use by the people who will be using it (not computer experts)?
- Is good documentation available? That is, are the instructions which explain the program complete, accurate, and easy-to-use?

Marketing

- What does the program do?
- What type of people would want this program?
- Will enough people buy it at the expected selling price?

If you believe your program looks good against these considerations, write to companies that produce and market programs. Outline what your program will do, but do not give details. If the company is interested, it will contact you. You should ask the company to sign a confidential agreement before you provide details.

Programming shareware. If you have written a computer program that you believe others would buy, consider marketing it yourself as "shareware." See Catalog C4 for further details on this interesting approach.

Inventing

In spite of stories of inventors being set for life because of one successful idea, inventing is a difficult way for a person to make money. Most inventions are developed by company employees, not independent inventors. On the other hand, through a combination of creativity and diligence, independent inventors have made it. For an excellent book, look for *The Inventor's Handbook*, by Robert Park, published by Betterway Publications, P.O. Box 219, Crozet, VA 22932.

Securing a patent. A patent is a very important part of your ability to sell an idea to a manufacturer. The U.S. government issues a patent that gives an inventor complete ownership of the idea for a specific period—for example, 17 years for mechanical or electrical patents. With a patent, no manufacturer can produce the idea without the inventor's permission. For that permission, the manufacturer pays the inventor a set amount or a royalty depending on the number of units sold.

The patent office examines an invention from several aspects before it grants a patent.

- **It must be a good idea.** It must be <u>new</u> and it must be <u>useful</u>. The test for newness is accomplished by searching previous patents for the same idea ("prior art"). While the patent office will perform its own search, you would be wise to pay an expert to conduct an early search for you. This could prevent you from wasting a great deal of time and money on an old idea.

  The invention must be useful—have a purpose. This old adage, "Necessity is the mother of invention," provides an excellent definition.

- **You must demonstrate that the idea will work—that it is feasible.** It is not enough to say, "I have a great idea. Why not make a car that uses water for fuel?" This is wishing—not inventing. To meet patent requirements, the invention must be "reduced to practice" (patent office words). That is, you must show how your invention works. In many cases, all you have to provide is a detailed explanation of how your invention works. However, if the patent office has doubts, you may have to provide a working model.

You should be aware that the patent application process can be costly and time-consuming. It can take from one to three years, and much longer if the patent office is not in agreement with your claims. Depending on the complexity of your patent, you could be well beyond the $1000 dollar limit of this book. Expenses can increase rapidly because of development costs, model making, searches of prior patents, and patent attorney fees.

A company considering buying an invention will have questions about the patent, but will analyze other factors as well. For example:

- **Can it be manufactured?** Can the product be made at a cost that will give a fair profit? Many patents have failed this test.

- **Can it be marketed successfully?** Does the product fit into the company's product line? How many products can be sold and at what price? These estimates will affect manufacturing costs.

- **Will it be profitable?** This is the famous "bottom line." If the invention cannot achieve the required revenue and profit, the project is dead!

So what can you do?

There are things you can do on a limited budget if you are willing to spend your time and effort in place of money.

The idea behind this approach is to do as little as you can but still get some protection for your idea. Then, broadcast your idea to several manufacturers with the hope that at least one will be interested enough in your invention to pay some of the expenses. Here's how it works.

First, there is no getting around the fact that you need a good idea and you must know the idea will work. Keep thorough notes in a bound notebook and date all entries. When you have confidence that the idea will work, explain the idea to two people you trust and have them sign and date your notebook. This will establish a history of your activities that could be very important if your patent is challenged by someone.

In the meantime, write to the Patent Office, U.S. Department of Commerce, Washington, D.C. 20231, and request a copy of its free booklet, *Disclosure Document Program.* The booklet describes how the patent office can help you protect your idea even before you apply for a patent. You must prepare a "Record of Invention" describing your invention in a concise yet detailed manner. You then sign and date the record and have two witnesses read and sign it. Follow the instructions in the booklet and send copies to the patent office, along with a check for $10.

The disclosure document program does <u>not</u> replace filing for a patent. Its sole purpose is to provide you with official proof that you did invent something at a certain time. Now when you contact a manufacturer about your idea, you have established and protected your invention and invention date so that you can talk freely.

You should contact manufacturers that you believe might be interested in your invention. Spend time at your local library searching for candidates. Either the *Thomas Register of American Manufacturers* or *MacRae's Blue Book* would be a good place to start. Begin by searching for companies that manufacture products in the same family as yours. Within that group of companies, look for those that have the manufacturing capabilities needed to produce your invention. For example, if your invention is a plastic automobile accessory, your first consideration should be to look for companies that manufacture car accessories. As the second consideration, the companies should have plastic production capabilities.

Write to the companies you have selected. Do <u>not</u> send your idea, but explain that you have an invention that you believe would be of interest to them. Tell them you would be pleased to provide more details if they will send you instructions on how to submit an invention to them.

What the human mind can conceive and believe, it can accomplish -
David Sarnoff

C16 Promotional businesses

Description: You act as the coordinator of other people's activities to get things done. For example, you promote a flea market by finding a suitable place, getting exhibitors to show their wares, and advertising to get customers to attend. As you can see, there are a number of people and activities that have to be coordinated.

Concerns: Are you a good enough communicator and organizer to get a number of people involved to get things done?

To control costs, can you find inexpensive ways to adequately advertise and promote your project? If you need a meeting or show place, can you find an inexpensive one?

Is there adequate interest from people who would participate? If you must charge them for participating, will they pay the amount you are asking?

Are there enough potential customers?

Tips: Carefully plan your new adventure. Costs can quickly add up, and you can find yourself financially strapped. See Lesson 19 for ideas on budget planning and cash flow.

Before committing, do your homework. Talk to potential participants and customers to determine their interests in your project.

Examples:

Flea markets. Flea markets are becoming so popular that there may already be enough in your area. If not, this could be an excellent opportunity to start one. You will need a large, open area that people can easily reach. Look for a place or open field that is not used during the day. You must arrange to rent the space for the day. Since this is extra income for the owner, you should be able to get a good price. You may be able to pay a percentage of the profits rather than a fixed amount. You can purchase a manual that covers all aspects of flea markets from Heartland Press, P.O. Box 543, Fenton, MO 63026.

Art or craft shows. Though similar in nature to flea markets, most art or craft shows cannot be run as frequently. You may have to set them up in different communities to assure continued good attendance.

Operate clubs. There are many different types of clubs you can operate. In most cases, you will have to find an inexpensive place to hold club gatherings. Some excellent choices include church halls and meeting rooms at civic organizations such as your local YMCA. But be prepared to tie in your plans with those of the rooms' owners. Another possibility would be smaller hotels and motels which have large meeting rooms. If drinks can be served, some of these hotels will take a low fee for the room if they can run the bar and keeps its profits.

Singles clubs. There are <u>many</u> singles who never liked or who are tired of the "wild scene." They just want to meet other nice people in a friendly and relaxed setting. You can provide this place, but you have to have an approach to get people to come—and come back again and again. Here is a hint. Provide a way for people to have fun while easily getting to meet and know others. For example, one enterprising person has developed a short questionnaire on likes and dislikes for each person to fill out. He feeds this data into a computer and within minutes matches people with similar tastes. There is no guarantee that people will like their selected partners, but it is a great "ice-breaker."

Aerobic exercise classes. While there are many health clubs offering these classes, most require fairly expensive membership fees, which include the use of other club facilities. Many people only want the aerobics class. You can rent an appropriate room, charge considerably less than health clubs, and be in business in a short time. This is one of the least expensive franchises available: Jazzercize, Inc., 2808 Roosevelt St., Carlsbad, CA 92008.

> **Dance clubs**. As new dances become popular, there is always a group of people eager to learn them. At the same time, old styles such as square dancing continue to be popular. By providing a large room, music, and instructions for those who need them, you can offer good entertainment and make money at the same time.

Community cookbooks. Look in any bookstore. Every year, cookbooks are sold by the hundreds of thousands, and I am sure this interest will continue forever. You can take advantage of this interest by promoting your own cookbook without preparing a single recipe. Here's how. Go to any organization wanting to raise money, such as a church or P.T.A. For a portion of the profits, offer to produce a cookbook of the favorite recipes of its members. (If you are active in your neighborhood, you can produce a neighborhood cookbook in the same way, without going to an organization. This way, you keep all the profits.) There are printers that specialize in producing this type of book. They can give you a great deal of help and advice. One such company is Fundcraft, 410 Hwy 72 W., P.O. Box 340, Collierville, TN 38017.

Sell advertisements on rental video tapes. One enterprising company is offering a unique program. You contact local video tape renters and offer to ease their expenses by placing advertisements on their video tapes. You then contact local businesses that might be interested in placing small ads on the tapes, which get seen by a number of browsers and renters. Contact Video/AD, 201 N. Tehama St., Suite D, P.O. Box 111, Willows, CA 95988.

Booklets for real estate agents. Real estate agents are among the first people to greet newcomers to an area. As such, they are in a good position to answer many of the practical questions newcomers might have. One way to do this is through a booklet with information about the area, plus advertisements from local merchants and services. You secure the ads, have the booklets printed and provide them free to the realtors. They can then distribute the booklets as their own. There are companies that will help you to get into this business by offering guidance and then printing the booklets. Here are two such companies: Advest Advertising, 111 S. Olive St., Suite 516, Media, PA 19063, and Homestead Publications of America, 2443 Fillmore St., Suite 329, San Francisco, CA 94115.

Give away fitness measuring machines. Here is a clever way to get in on the continuing fitness boom. You contact health clubs and offer them the use of an exercise device that measures overall fitness. How can you give away these rather expensive machines? You sell a few advertisements that attach to the machine in front of the user as measurements are being taken. The money from those ads more than pays for the device. Interested? Contact Bodylog, 34 Maple Ave., P.O. Box 8, Armonk, N.Y. 10504.

Have youth groups sell for you. Kids of high school and college age are always looking for ways to make money. You can help with this program specifically designed to help youths to sell auto safety kits. Your activities are primarily to recruit candidates and supervise their work. Contact American Youth Enterprises, 128 N. Merritt Ave., P.O. Box 962, Salisbury, NC 28144.

Coordinate corporate golf outings. This is a good one for avid golfers. Many large companies hold golf outings for their customers and employees. The management of all aspects of a well-planned outing takes time and experience, and this is where you come in. By making all arrangements, from selecting a course to ordering prizes, you can assure a successful and enjoyable time for all participants. For a manual on this opportunity, write to Marshall & Associates, 3434 Vinings North Trail, Smyrna, GA 30080.

Live all you can; it's a mistake not to - Henry James

C17 Businesses you can start if you have certain equipment

Description: Selecting an opportunity may depend on the tools and equipment you would need. To stay within the dollar limits of this book, you cannot afford to start a business by buying expensive equipment. However, if you already own the equipment, you certainly can use it in your new business.

I will give some ideas on how you can make money if you own certain equipment, including, a truck, a car, a camera, a personal computer, a sewing machine, or access to a big room.

Concerns: Is the equipment of good quality and reliable enough so that you can depend on it when you need it?

Are there any insurance implications if you use the equipment for business? This is especially important if you use a vehicle or part of your home.

Tips: There may be some substantial tax benefits if you can depreciate the equipment (see Lesson 27). The equipment need not be new for you to get these benefits. Best to see your tax advisor about this.

If you continue to use the equipment for personal use as well as for the business, you may have to keep records of usage to get the maximum tax benefits.

Remember, using the equipment more frequently will make it subject to more breakdowns. Watch the equipment carefully and schedule preventative maintenance during quiet times to keep it in top shape when needed.

Examples:

If you have a truck

Basement, attic, garage cleaning
Hauling
Light moving
Snow plowing
Recycling
Delivery service
Yard and garden work

If you have a car

Visit shut-ins
Deliver home meals to shut-ins
Courier and delivery service for businesses
Home delivery from restaurants
After-school transportation for children
Limousine service

If you have a camera

Take pictures of personal property for insurance records
Pet photos
Weddings
"Free" photos—then sell enlargements
Dances and parties

Posing with cutouts of famous people. This requires an instant camera and the ability to go wherever there are many people, such as at a fair or tourist attraction. Get a full-size enlargement of a famous person, like the president. Mount it on a board and cut around the outline. Have customers pose next to it.

If you have a video camera

Weddings and parties
Local sports events
Use with lessons for golf, tennis, etc.
Local theater productions

If you have a sewing machine

Custom-made clothing
Mending and alterations
Soft toys and stuffed animals
Drapes
Repair upholstery
Monogramming
Get a contract to do alterations for local cleaners and clothing stores
Sew on emblems and make alterations for sporting goods stores

If you own a personal computer

Bookkeeping
Prepare mailing labels
Data entry
Singles matching
Apartment finding
Roommate matching
Mortgage reduction

If you own a laser printer with your personal computer

Word processing service
Resume writing
Brochure and flyer preparation
Menu preparation
Sales letters

If you have a large room

There are a number of activities you can promote if you have a large room available to you, such as your basement, a barn, or a room you can rent at low cost. Churches may be a good source, since many have meeting and class rooms that are not used much of the time. YMCA and YWCA facilities are another good possibility. Here are a few examples of activities you can promote if there is a large room available:

Square dance clubs
Aerobics
Craft exhibits and sales
Art shows
Magic, puppet, and marionette shows

After-school programs for children
Adult classes on numerous subjects
"Swap-shop" for sporting goods or outgrown children's clothing.

A wise man makes more opportunity than he finds - Francis Bacon

Section J

Your final checkout

Exercise 9 | A checklist for your Mini-biz

Instructions

This checklist is designed to help you identify important startup activities <u>before</u> you start your Mini-biz. It is quite long because it covers a wide range of business types. Don't worry. Many activities will not apply to you and your Mini-biz. Use a pencil in case you want to make a change. Here's what to do:

1. Go through the complete list carefully. In the left column, check the boxes for those activities that apply to you and your business. A box like ❑ indicates an activity that will be VERY IMPORTANT to a large number of businesses. Give these extra consideration as you check activities for <u>your</u> business.

2. If you check a box in the left column, use the right box to check off activities you have completed or have under control.

3. If you want more information, the number following most questions tells you which lessons and exercises to review.

4. When you are finished, **for every left box with a check you should have checked its right box as well.** If not, you have an activity that needs more attention before you commit to starting your Mini-biz.

Personal checklist

Your Mini-biz needs this.
It is completed or under control.

❑ ☐ Are you the "right person" for the Mini-biz you plan? (13, Ex. 1)
❑ ☐ Have you estimated the time requirements of your Mini-biz? (13, Ex. 2)
☐ ☐ If married, does your spouse agree with your plans for a Mini-biz? (13, Ex. 1)
❑ ☐ Do you have the required technical skills and knowledge? (13, Ex. 1)
☐ ☐ Can you handle the bookkeeping part of the business? (26)
☐ ☐ Do you know where you can go to get help or advice, if you need it? (14)
Do you understand your obligations for:
☐ ☐ Federal personal taxes? (26)
☐ ☐ State and local personal taxes? (26)
☐ ☐ Social Security self-employment taxes? (26)

Exercise 9 Checklist

Your business checklist

Your Mini-biz needs this.
It is completed or under control.

- ☐ ☐ Are economic times in your area okay to start your Mini-biz? (13, Ex. 1)
- ☐ ☐ Have you selected the legal form of your business? (21)
- ☐ ☐ If a partnership, do you work well with your future partner? (21)
- ☐ ☐ Do you know where you will conduct your business (at home, at fairs, at customer's home or office, etc.)? (13, Ex. 1, and 19, Ex. 6)
- ☐ ☐ Do you need zoning approval? (24)
- ☐ ☐ Do you have a name for your company? (29)
- ☐ ☐ Do you need to register your company name? (29)

Do you need any of the following?

- ☐ ☐ Permits? (23)
- ☐ ☐ Business licenses? (23)
- ☐ ☐ Resale permit? (26)
- ☐ ☐ Business cards? (30)
- ☐ ☐ Business stationery? (30)
- ☐ ☐ Sales slips or sales books? (30 and 36)
- ☐ ☐ Business telephone? (30)
- ☐ ☐ Telephone answering machine? (30)
- ☐ ☐ Special tools and equipment to start? (13, Ex. 2)
- ☐ ☐ Vehicle for your Mini-biz?
- ☐ ☐ Lawyer? (21, 38, Catalog C15)
- ☐ ☐ Accountant? (26, 27, 28, 36, 38)
- ☐ ☐ Insurance for the business use of a vehicle? (25)
- ☐ ☐ Insurance for the business use of part of your home? (25)
- ☐ ☐ Liability insurance? (25)

- ☐ ☐ If you need products or supplies, do you have good sources? (30)
- ☐ ☐ Have you set up a business bank account? (22)
- ☐ ☐ Do you have a bookkeeping system in place? (36)
- ☐ ☐ Do you have a system to record business use of your vehicle? (28)

Exercise 9 Checklist

Your marketing checklist

Your Mini-biz needs this.
It is completed or under control.

☐ ☐ Can you describe your typical customers? (16)
☐ ☐ Do you see a significant need for your product or service?
☐ ☐ Do you believe there are enough customers in your business area to make your business profitable? (19, Ex. 6)
☐ ☐ Can you name your competitors? (17)
☐ ☐ Do you know why customers will buy from you? (19, Ex. 6)
☐ ☐ Do you know how to price your products or services? (31)
☐ ☐ Are your prices competitive? (17 and 31)
☐ ☐ Do you know where you will be selling? (19, Ex. 6)
☐ ☐ Do you have a sales approach? (32)
☐ ☐ Do you know how you intend to advertise? (33 and 34, Ex. 8)
☐ ☐ Do you know how you will get publicity? (34, Ex. 8)

Your financial checklist

☐ ☐ Do you have goals for the business? (13, Ex. 3)
☐ ☐ Can you cover your startup expenses? (19, Ex.5)
☐ ☐ Will your Mini-biz require you to spend money each month? (19, Ex. 5)
☐ ☐ If yes, do you see money coming in to pay those bills? (19, Ex. 5)
☐ ☐ Do you have a source for more money if you need it? (13, Ex. 2)

If you hire employees (All from Lesson 28)

☐ ☐ Do you have to apply for Employer Identification Number?
☐ ☐ Did you check with your state revenue department for state tax requirements?
☐ ☐ Did you check on your state's unemployment tax collection requirements?

Have you set up a system for:
☐ ☐ Payroll?
☐ ☐ Social Security recording?
☐ ☐ Federal Unemployment Taxes?
☐ ☐ Workers' Compensation Insurance?

It takes 20 years to become an overnight success - Eddie Cantor